Significant Business Results

Ten Sales Secrets That Your Competitors Know and Use!

Significant Business Results

Ten Sales Secrets That Your Competitors Know and Use!

by Franne McNeal, MBA
Significant Business Results Coach

COPYRIGHT AND DISCLAIMER

INTRODUCTION

By opening this book you have already taken an important step towards increasing your success as an entrepreneur. Congratulations on your commitment to enhance your marketing, sales and business skills.

When I started to write this book, I found myself with an enormous amount of useful marketing material, so I've included principles and lessons from my professional and academic experiences to help you access and activate more sales opportunities than you imagined.

I am a serial entrepreneur with corporate expertise that spans four industries, seven positions and over thirty years in business. As a junior at Princeton University, I launched a successful catering recruiting business for student bartenders and wait staff and never looked back. When I was 26 years old, I was the youngest person ever to be awarded a training contract with the City of Pittsburgh; and successfully financed my 18-computer training room in one month.

In corporate leadership positions at Strategic Computer Assistance Inc, Mellon Bank, FMC, and SmithKline Beecham, as well as Vice President of Training and Development at PNC Financial Services, I led restructuring initiatives that resulted in over $1M in measurable savings.

In 2001, I created an entrepreneur and executive business coaching practice. My clients were facing business challenges, and needed a trusted advisor with an entrepreneurial perspective, market savvy, and insightful questions to foster business growth and accountability. My clients needed and a Significant Business Results Coach who understood their goals and challenges, had access to networks and resources, and who could help them grow their business with more clients, more revenue and more profits.

I help my clients grow brand value, create growth strategies, identify niche revenue streams, and increase profits by leveraging people, performance, and process.

The sales strategies in this book, when implemented, are guaranteed to make you more money with less effort. These strategies have helped businesses just like yours, including your competitors, make hundreds of thousands of dollars.

As you read this book, remember to apply the heart of the principles, the underlying lessons and strategies, in your business. The best time to start is NOW, not tomorrow, not next week or next year.

Significantly yours in success,

Franne McNeal, MBA
Significant Business Results Coach
Franne@SBizResults.com
www.SBizResults.com

Are you ready to increase your sales, cash flow and profits?

Hire a Significant Business Results Coach.
Get faster and smarter business growth.

Acquire the best marketing resources at www.SBizResults.com
Bonus: Seven-day access to a business building membership site.

DEDICATION

I would like to dedicate this book to my grandfather, George Edward McNeal Sr. I am inspired by the creativity and perseverance he put towards his small businesses. I have taken many of the lessons he learned and put them into this book.

Thank you to my parents George and Lynnette, and my sisters Nancy, Jacqueline, and Marilyn for encouraging my entrepreneurial spirit.

Special thanks to my business team: Everaldo Gallimore, Yvonne Tucker, John L. Thompson, Michele Ortmann and LaSonya Thompson.

Significantly,
Franne McNeal

CONTENTS

Define Your Target Market

What is a Target Market?

Many businesses can't answer the question, "Who is your target market?" They have often made the fatal assumption that *everyone* will want to purchase their product or service with the right marketing strategy.

A target market is simply the group of customers or clients who will purchase a specific product or service. This group of people has something in common--often age, gender, hobbies, or location.

Your target market, then, are the people who will buy your offering. This includes both existing and potential customers, all of whom are motivated to do one of three things:

- Fulfill a need
- Solve a problem

- Satisfy a desire

To build, maintain, and grow your business, you need to know who your customers are, what they do, what they like, and why they will buy your product or service. Getting this wrong – or not taking the time to get it right – will cost you time, money, and potentially the success of your business.

Knowing Your Target Market

Knowledge and understanding of your target market is the keystone in the arch of your business. Without it, your product or service positioning, pricing, marketing strategy, and eventually your business could very quickly fall apart.

If you don't intimately know your target market, you run the risk of making mistakes when it comes to establishing pricing, product mix, or service packages. Your marketing strategy will lack direction, and produce mediocre results, at best. Even if your marketing message and unique selling proposition (USP) are clear, and your brochure is perfectly designed, it means nothing unless it arrives in the hands (or ears) of the right people.

Determining your target market takes time and careful diligence. While it often starts with a best guess, assumptions cannot be relied on and research is required to confirm original ideas. Your target market is not always your ideal market.

Once you build an understanding of who your target market is, keep up with your market research. Having your finger on the pulse of their motivations and drivers – which naturally change – will help you to anticipate needs or wants and evolve your business.

Within your local community there should be a library with a business research department, so contact the librarian for assistance.

Types of Markets

1. Consumer

The Consumer Market includes those general consumers who buy products and services for personal use, or for use by family and friends. This is the market category that you or I fall into when we're shopping for groceries or clothes, seeing a movie in the theatre, or going out for lunch. Retailers focus on this market category when marketing their goods or services.

2. Institutional

The Institutional Market serves society and provides products or services for the benefit of society. This includes hospitals, non-profit organizations, government organizations, schools, and universities. Members of the Institutional Market purchase products to use in the provision of services to people in their care.

3. Business to Business (B2B)

The B2B Market is just what it seems to be: businesses that purchase the products and services of other business to run their operations. These purchases can include products that are used to manufacture other products (raw or technical), products that are needed for daily operations (such as office supplies), or services (such as accounting, shredding, shipping, and legal).

4. Reseller

This market can also be called the "Intermediary Market" because it consists of businesses that act as channels for goods and services between other markets. Goods are purchased and sold for a profit – without any alterations. Members of this market include wholesalers, retailers, resellers, and distributors.

Determining Your Target Market

Product / Service Investigation

The process for determining your target market starts by examining exactly what your offering is, and what the average customer's motivation for purchasing it is.

- Does your offering meet a basic need?

- Does your offering serve a particular want?

- Does your offering fulfill a desire?

- What is the lifecycle of your product / service?

- What is the availability of your offering?

- What is the cost of your average customer's purchase?

- What is the lifecycle of your offering?

- How many times or how often will your customers purchase your offering?

- Do you foresee any upcoming changes (positive or negative) in your industry or region that may affect the sale of your offering?

Market Investigation

1. On the ground

Spend some time on the ground researching who your target market might be. If you're thinking about opening a coffee shop, hang out in the neighborhood at different times of the day to get a sense of the people who live, work, and play in the neighborhood. Notice their age, gender, clothing, and any other indications of income and activities.

2. At the competition

Who is your direct competitor targeting? Is there a small niche that is being missed? Observing the clientele of your competition can help to build understanding of your target market, regardless of whether it is the same or opposite. For example, if you own a children's clothing boutique and the majority of middle-class mothers shop at the local department store, you may wish to focus on higher-income families as your target market.

3. Online

Many cities and towns – or at least regions – have demographic information available online. Research the ages, incomes, occupations, and other key pieces of information about the people who live in the area you operate your business. From this data, you will gain an understanding of the size of your total potential market.

4. With existing customers

Talk to your existing customers through focus groups or surveys. This is a great way to gather demographic and behavioral information, as well as genuine feedback about product or service quality, and other information that will be useful in a business or marketing strategy.

Who is Your Market?

Based on your product / service and market investigations, you will be able to piece together a basic picture of your target market, and some of their general characteristics. Select the appropriate form, from the following four pages, and make notes as a way to gain a clearer vision of your most realistic target market. Pages 11 and 12 are completed sample forms.

Consumer Target Market

Market Type:	**Consumer**
Gender:	☐ Male ☐ Female
Age Range:	
Purchase Motivation:	☐ Meet a Need ☐ Serve a Want ☐ Fulfill a Desire
Activities:	
Income Range:	
Marital Status:	
Location:	☐ Neighborhood ☐ City ☐ Region ☐ Country
Other Notes:	

Institutional Target Market

Market Type:	Institutional
Institution Type:	☐ Hospital ☐ Non-profit ☐ School ☐ University ☐ Charity ☐ Government ☐ Church
Purchase Motivation:	☐ Operational Need ☐ Client Want ☐ Client Desire
Purpose of Institution:	
Institution's Client Base:	
Size:	
Location:	☐ Neighborhood ☐ City ☐ Region ☐ Country
Other Notes:	

Business to Business Target Market

Market Type:	**Business to Business (B2B)**
Company Size:	
Number of Employees:	
Purchase Motivation:	☐ Operations Need ☐ Strategy ☐ Functionality
Annual Revenue:	
Industry:	
Location(s):	
Purpose of Business:	
People, Culture & Values:	
Other Notes:	

Reseller Target Market

Market Type:	**Reseller**
Industry:	
Client Base:	
Purchase Motivation:	☐ Operations Need ☐ Strategy ☐ Functionality
Annual Revenue:	
Age:	
Location:	☐ Neighborhood ☐ City ☐ Region ☐ Country
Other Notes:	

Completed Sample: Target Market (Consumer)

Business: Baby Clothing Boutique **Market Type:** Consumer **Gender:** Women **Marital Status:** Married	**Business Purpose:** Meet a need (provide clothing for infants and children aged 0 to 5 years). Serve a want (clothing is brand name only, and has a higher price point than the competition).
Market Observations: Located on Main Street of AnyTown, a street that is seeing many new boutiques open up, proximate to the main shopping mall, two blocks from popular mid-range restaurant that is busy at lunch.	**Industry Predictions:** Large number of new housing developments in the city and surrounding areas, two new schools in construction Expect to see an influx of new families move to town from AnyCity.
Competition Observations: Baby clothing also available at two local department stores, and one second-hand shop on opposite side of town.	**Online Research:** Half of Anytown's population is female, and 25% have children under the age of fifteen years. AnyTown's population is expected to increase by 32% within three years. The average household income for AnyTown is $75,000 annually.
TARGET MARKET: The target market is married mothers with children under five years old, between the ages of 25 and 45, who have recently moved to AnyTown from Anycity, and have a household income of at least $100K annually.	

11

Completed Sample: Target Market (B2B)

Business: Confidential Paper Shredding	**Target Business Size:** Small to medium
Market Type: B2B (Business to Business)	**Target Business Revenue:** $500K to $1M
Business Purpose: Meet an operations need (provide confidential on-site shredding services for business documents).	**Target Business Type:** Produce or handle a variety of sensitive paper documentation accountants, lawyers, real estate agents, etc.
Market Observations: There are two main areas of office buildings and industrial warehouses in AnyCity, Three more office towers are being constructed and will be completed this year.	**Industry Predictions:** The professional sector is seeing revenue growth of 24% over last year, which indicates increased client billing and staff recruitment.
Competition Observations: One confidential shredding company serves the region, covering AnyCity and the surrounding towns. Provides regular (weekly or biweekly) service, but does not have the capacity to handle large volumes at one time.	**Online Research:** AnyCity's biggest employment sectors are: manufacturing, tourism, food services, and professional services.
TARGET MARKET: The target market is small to medium sized businesses in the professional sector with annual revenue of $500K to $1M who require both regular and infrequent large volume paper shredding services.	

Segmenting Your Market

Your market segments are the groups within your target market – broken down by a determinant in one of the following four categories:

- Demographics
- Psychographics
- Geographics
- Behaviors

Segmenting your target market into several more specific groups allows you to further tailor your marketing campaign and more specifically position your product or service. You may wish to divide your ad campaign into four sections, and target four specific markets with messages that will most resonate with the audience.

For example, the baby clothing store may choose to segment its target market by psychographics, or lifestyle. If the larger target market is *married females with children under five, between the ages of 25 and 45, who have a household income of at least $100K annually*, it can be broken down into following lifestyle segments:

- Fitness-oriented mothers
- Career-oriented mothers
- New mothers

With these three categories, unique marketing messages can be created that speak to the hot-buttons of each segment. The more accurate and specific you can make communications with your target market, the greater impact you will have on your revenues.

Market Segmentation Variables

Demographic	Psychographic	Geographic	Behavioristic
Age	Personality	Region	Brand Loyalty
Income	Lifestyle	Country	Product Usage
Gender	Values	City	Purchase Frequency
Generation	Attitude	Area	Profitability
Nationality	Motivation	Neighborhood	Readiness to Buy
Ethnicity	Activities	Density	User Status
Marital Status	Interests	Climate	
Family Size			
Occupation			
Religion			
Language			
Education			
Employment Type			
Housing Type			
Home Owner			
Political Affiliation			

Understanding Your Target Market

Once you have determined who your market is, make a point of learning everything you can about them. You need to have a strong understanding of who they are, what they like, where they shop, why they buy, and how they spend their time. Remind yourself that you may *think* you know your market, but until you have verified the information, you'll be driving your marketing strategy blind.

Also be aware that markets change, just like people. Just because you knew your market when you started your business ten years ago doesn't mean you know it now. Regular market research is part of any successful business plan, and a great habit to start.

Types of Market Research

1. Surveys

The simplest way to gather information from your clients or target market is through a survey. You can craft a questionnaire full of questions about your product, service, market demographics, buyer motivations, and so on. Plus, anonymous surveys will produce the most accurate information, since names are not attached to the results or specific comments.

Depending on the purpose—whether it is to gather demographic information, product or service feedback, or other data—there are a number of ways to administer a survey.

2. Telephone

Telephone surveys are a more time-consuming option, but have the benefit of live communication with your target market. Generally, it is best to have a third party conduct this type of survey to gather the most honest feedback. This is the method that market researchers use for polling, which is highly reliable. Be aware of local or state laws regarding telephone surveys.

3. Online

Online surveys are the easiest to administer yourself. There a many web-based services that quickly and easily allow to you custom create your survey, and send it to your email marketing list. These services can also analyze, summarize, and interpret the results on your behalf. Keep in mind that the results include only those who are motivated to respond, which may slant your results.

4. Paper-based

Paper surveys are seldom used, and can prove to be an inefficient method. Like online surveys, your results are based on the feedback of those who were motivated for one reason or another to respond. However, the time and effort involved in taking the survey, filing it out, and returning it to your place of business may deter people from participating.

Keep in mind that surveys can be complex to administer, and consume more time and resources than you had planned. If you have the budget, consider hiring a professional market research firm to lead or assist with the process. This will also ensure that the methodology is standard practice, and will garner the most accurate results.

5. Website analysis

Tracking your website traffic (analytics) is an excellent way to research your existing and potential customer's interests and behavior. Analytics helps ensure that the design, structure and content of your website is catering to the people who use it, and the people you want to use it.

User friendly website traffic analytics programs can easily show you who is visiting your site, where they are from, and what pages of your site they are viewing.

Services like Google Analytics can tell you what page they arrive at, where they click to, how much time they spend on each page, and on which page they leave the site.

This is powerful (and free) information to have in your market research, and easy to monitor monthly or weekly, depending on the needs of your business.

6. **List additional ideas**

   a. _____

   b. _____

   c. _____

   d. _____

   e. _____

Consumer Behavior

If you do not have the budget to conduct your own professional market research, you can use existing resources on consumer behavior. While this data may not be specific to your region or city, general consumer research is actual data that can be helpful in confirming assumptions that you may have made about your target market.

Your customer loyalty program or point of sale system may also be of help in tracking customer purchases and identifying trends in purchase behavior. If you can track who is buying, what they're buying, and how often they're buying, you'll have an arsenal of powerful insight into your existing client base.

Focus Groups

Focus groups look at the psychographic and behavioristic aspects of your target market. Groups of six to twelve people are gathered and asked general and specific questions about their purchase motivations and behaviors. These questions can relate to your business in particular, or to the general industry.

Focus group sessions can also be time consuming to organize and facilitate, so consider hiring the services of a professional market research firm. You may also receive more honest information if a third party is asking the questions and receiving the responses from focus group participants.

For cost savings, consider partnering with an associate in the same industry who is not a direct competitor, and who would benefit from the same market data.

Action Questions from Chapter 1

A. Target Market

Who is your target market?

Why will they buy?

What do they have in common?

Action Questions from Chapter 1, continued

B. Market Investigation

Where can find information about your target market?

C. Clarify Your Market

Which characteristics are important within your target market?

D. Market Segmentation Variables

What are the market segmentation variables?

E. Market Research

What type of market research will be most effective?

What additional market research do you need to conduct?

F. Consumer Behavior

Where can you acquire consumer behavior data?

Who has access to and/or wants similar market data?

G. Next Step

What "doable" next step will facilitate significant business results?

2

Create a Powerful Offer

The Power Offer is Undeniable

Your offer is the foundation of your marketing campaign.

Get it right and everything else will fall into place. Your headline will grab readers, your copy will sing, your ad layout will hardly matter, and you will have customers running to your door.

Get it wrong, and even the best looking, best-written campaign will sink like the Titanic.

A powerful offer is an irresistible offer. It's an offer that gets your audience frothing at the mouth and clamoring over each other all the way to your door, an offer that makes your readers pick up the phone and open their wallets.

Irresistible offers make your potential customers think, "I'd be crazy not to take him up on that," or "An offer like this doesn't come around very often." They instill a sense of emotion, of desire, and ultimately, urgency.

Make it easy for customers to purchase from you the first time, and spend your time keeping them coming back.

When you get it right, everything else will fall into place.

The Crux of Your Marketing Campaign

As you work your way through this book, you will find that nearly every chapter discusses the importance of a powerful offer, as related to your marketing strategy or promotional campaign.

There's a reason for this. The powerful offer is more often than not the reason a customer will open their wallet. It is how you generate leads, and then convert them into loyal customers. The more dramatic, unbelievable, and valuable the offer is, the more dramatic and unbelievable the response will be.

Many companies spend thousands of dollars on impressive marketing campaigns in glossy magazines and big city newspapers. They send massive direct mail campaigns on a regular basis; yet they don't receive an impressive or massive response rate.

These companies don't understand that simply providing features and benefits of their product or service is not enough to get customers to act, pick up the phone, visit the store right now or click through on an offer.

Your powerful, irresistible offer can:

- Increase leads
- Drive traffic to your website or business
- Move old product
- Convert leads into customers
- Build your customer database

What Makes a Powerful Offer?

A powerful offer is one that makes the most people respond, and take action. It gets people running to spend money on your product or service.

Powerful offers nearly always have an element of *urgency* and of *scarcity*. They give your audience a reason to act immediately, instead of put it off until a later date.

Urgency relates to time. The offer is only available until a certain date, during a certain period of the day, or if you act within a few hours of seeing the ad. The customer needs to act now to take advantage of the offer.

Scarcity related to quantity. There are only a certain number of customers who will be able to take advantage of the offer. There may be a limited number of spaces, a limited number of products, or simply a limited number of people the business will provide the offer to. Again, this requires that customers act immediately to reap the high value for low cost.

Characteristics of a Powerful Offer

1. Offer great value

Customers perceive the offer as having great value – more than a single product on its own, or the product at its regular price. It is clear that the offer takes the reader's needs and wants into consideration.

2. Makes sense to the reader

They are simple and easy to understand, if read quickly. Avoid percentages – use half off or two for one instead of 50% off. There are no "catches" or requirements, no fine print.

3. Seem logical

The offer doesn't come out of thin air. There is a logical reason behind it: a holiday, end of season, anniversary celebration, or new product. People get suspicious of offers that seem "too good to be true" and have no apparent purpose.

4. Provide a premium

The offer provides something extra to the customer, like a free gift, or free product or service. They feel they are getting something extra for no extra cost. Premiums are perceived to have more value than discounts.

Remember that when your target market reads your offer, they will be asking the following questions:

- What are you offering me?
- What is in it for me?
- What makes me sure I can believe you?
- How much do I have to pay for it?

The Most Powerful Types of Offers

Decide what kind of offer will most effectively achieve your objectives. Are you trying to generate leads, convert customers, build a database, move old product off the shelves, or increase sales?

Consider what type of offer will be of most value to your ideal customers. What offer will make them act quickly?

1. Free offer

This type of offer asks customers to act immediately in exchange for something for free. This is a good strategy to use to build a customer database or mailing list. Offer a free consultation, free consumer report, or other item of low cost to you, but of high perceived value to the customer.

You can also advertise the value of the item you are offering for free. For example, act now and you'll receive a free consultation, worth $75 dollars. This will dramatically increase your lead generation, and allow you to focus on conversion when the customer comes through the door or picks up the phone.

2. The value added offer

Add additional services or products that cost you very little, and combine them with other items to increase their attractiveness. This increases the perception of value in the customer's mind, which will justify increasing the price of a product or service without incurring extra hard costs to your business.

3. Package offer

Package your products or services together in a logical way to increase the perceived value, as a whole. Discount the value of the package by a small margin and position it as a "start-up kit" or "special package." By packaging goods of mixed values, you will be able to close more high-value sales. For example: including a free desk-jet printer with every computer purchase.

4. Premium offer

Offer a bonus product or service with the purchase of another. This strategy will serve your bottom line much better than discounting. This includes two for one offers, offers that include free gifts, and in-store credit with purchases over a specific dollar amount.

5. Urgency offer

As I mentioned above, offers that include an element of urgency enjoy a better response rate, as there is a reason for your customers to act immediately. Give the offer a deadline or limit the number of spots available.

6. Guarantee offer

Offer to take the risk of making a purchase away from your customers. Guarantee the performance or results of your product or service, and offer to compensate the customer with their money back if they are not satisfied. This will help overcome any fear or reservations about your product, and make it more likely for your leads to become customers.

7. List additional ideas

a. _____

b. _____

Create Your Powerful Offer

1. Pick a single product or service

Focus on only one product or service – or one product or service *type* – at a time. This will keep your offer clear, simple, and easy to understand. This can be an area of your business that you wish to grow, or an old product that you need to move off the shelves.

2. Decide what you want your customers to do

What are you looking to achieve from your offer?

If you want to generate more leads, then you'll need your customers to contact you. If you want to quickly sell old product, you'll need your customers to come into the store and buy it.

Be clear about your call to action, and state it clearly in your offer. Do you want them to visit your website? Sign up for your newsletter? How long do they have to act?

3. Dream up the biggest, best offer

First, think of the biggest, best things that you can offer your customers – regardless of cost and ability. Don't limit yourself to a single type of offer, combine several types of offers to increase value. Offer a premium, plus a guarantee with a package offer. Then adjust for reality.

4. Run the numbers

Finally, make sure the offer will leave you with some profit – or at least allow you to break even. You don't want to publish an outrageous offer that will generate a tremendous number of leads but leave you broke. Remember that each customer has an acquisition cost, as well as a lifetime value. The amount of their first purchase may allow you to break even, but the amount of their subsequent purchases may make you a lovely profit.

5. List additional ideas

a. _____

b. _____

c. _____

d. _____

e. _____

f. _____

g. _____

h. _____

i. _____

Action Questions from Chapter 2

A. Undeniable Powerful Offer

What will make them think: "I'd be crazy not buy this?"

What will create a sense of emotion, desire, and urgency?

B. Powerful Offer Characteristics

What will you do create "great value'?

What will you say that "makes the most sense" to your reader?

What will you say that is "logical" to your reader?

What will your offer as your "premium"?

C. Powerful Offer Types

Which offer type will have the most impact for your business?

D. Create a Powerful Offer

Which single product or service will you choose?

What do you want your customers to do?

What is your biggest and best offer?

E. Next Step

What "doable" next step will facilitate significant business results?

3

Use Testimonials for Social Proof

The Power of Testimonials

Testimonials are simply the single most powerful asset you can have in your marketing toolkit. When your customers tell others about the benefits of choosing your business, it is a thousand times more powerful than the same words from your mouth.

The words and opinions of others motivate people to spend money every day. From celebrity endorsements on TV and in magazines to casual conversations with friends, decisions about what product or service to buy – and what brand or provider – are heavily influenced by those who have purchased before.

Why? There are several reasons. Many people have an inherent distrust of salespeople, and a healthy skepticism toward marketing materials. Others are bombarded with choice and are looking for some sense of security in their purchase decision.

Testimonials build the credibility of your business, break down natural barriers, and create a sense of trust for the consumer. They have an incredible ability to persuade customers to buy, and to buy from you. Think about the last time someone recommended a brand of laundry detergent, a bottle of wine, or a plumber to you. Their positive experience had more of an impact on your decision to buy than any advertisement or discount.

When it comes to spending money, people want to know that someone else has bought before, and they want to know that the product or service has delivered the promised results. A testimonial for your business is worth more than any copywriter, clever ad slogan, or sales pitch. Testimonials are "social" proof that people know, like and trust your product, service and business.

Customers Who Give Testimonials

When people put their name and reputation on paper to endorse something, it creates a sense of loyalty; if questioned, they will back their decision, even if they find later that their decision was wrong.

When someone is willing to endorse your product or service in writing, they have likely already started a word-of-mouth chain of verbal testimonials about their positive experience. Remember the last time you discovered a chiropractic miracle worker, or the fastest and cheapest drycleaner? Didn't you tell every one of your friends who could use the service?

By asking a customer for a testimonial, you are asking for their assistance in the growth of your business. When they feel they are truly helping and participating in the development of your company, their sense of pride will mean continuous loyalty to your product or service.

11 Ways to Get Great Testimonials

Testimonials are powerful – no question. But how do you make sure that the quotes you get from your customers will bring you the most value? How do you ensure that your client will articulate your product's merits in a clear and easy to understand way? How do you make sure you can actually use their testimonials in your marketing materials?

Asking for testimonials requires more effort than merely soliciting general comments and praise. You want to ensure that your customer feels a sense of pride and loyalty in providing their opinion, and that their opinion will have an impact on potential buyers. Here are eleven proven ways to get great testimonials.

1. Don't wait!

Your customers are the happiest and most willing to help you within a day to a week from their purchase, so aim to secure the testimonial in this time period. Ask for the testimonial before they leave, and make sure you have all their contact details to follow-up. This also ensures that you stay on top of your testimonial recruitment!

2. Get specific

Specific testimonials are more believable. The more specific you can have your customer be, the stronger and more impactful the testimonial will be. Remember the Sleep Country testimonials that referenced the little "booties" that their delivery men wore to keep carpets clean? Meaningful details get remembered. Ask for mention of things like time, dates, extraordinary customer service, and personal observations.

3. If you were the solution – what was the problem?

Testimonials that tell stories are more engaging. Ask clients to not only describe their experiences with your company, but also the negative experiences that led them to your door. If they can describe the struggles and challenges they were facing before receiving your service, the reader will likely be able to sympathize and resonate with similar struggles. This will motivate them to solve their problems with your solution.

4. Write the first draft

Make it easy for your clients. This technique is something you can offer someone who is hesitant to commit to writing a testimonial due to time constraints, or is procrastinating. Ask them to brainstorm a few notes that they want to include in their feedback, write them down, and string them into a concise testimonial for their review. All they have to do is review, print on their letterhead, sign, and mail back to you!

5. Include your marketing message or USP

Always ask your customers to include your unique selling proposition (USP) in the testimonial. For instance, if your USP includes exceptional customer service, same-day installation, and a money-back guarantee, then ask your customer to attest to those qualities.

6. A picture says…

Yes, you know the saying. But it's true. When readers attach an image of the speaker to words, the words are enlivened and have twice as much validity and impact. When readers see an image of a previous client using your product or service, their words and opinions are even more believable. You can take these simple pictures yourself – and take many so you have a selection to choose from. But make sure you in permission in writing to use the clients visual testimonial.

7. Credentials equal trust

As we mentioned, testimonials from credible sources have the most believability and impact. When you ask for a testimonial, make sure your customer states their expertise and credentials. If you sell custom orthotics, and can secure a solid testimonial from a doctor, then their words will be golden in your marketing materials.

8. Don't forget to ask permission

When you ask for testimonials, make sure you are clear that their words may be used in your marketing materials, including advertisements, website and in-store displays. This is a good time to thank them for their time and sincerity, and show your appreciation. Get a waiver signed for permission to use the testimonial.

9. Location, location...

Depending on the market reach for your business, the location of your customers is an important part of the believability of your testimonial. If you own a community-based business, when potential clients see you've made others happy just down their street, then they'll be motivated to use your service, too. If you own a regional business, then the cities and addresses of other happy customers can help communicate the reach of your service.

10. Testimonials are not surveys

Keep the purpose of your request in mind when you're asking for testimonials. Testimonials should be positive fodder for your advertising materials. Surveys are used to solicit meaningful (and often confidential) customer information to refine and improve your service. Testimonials are public statements, while surveys are often anonymous and can produce less-than-positive results.

11. Say thank you!

Thanking a customer for their time and effort in creating your testimonial is just plain good manners. It also increases loyalty and goodwill. This can be done via email, but sending a formal letter on your letterhead is a more meaningful approach.

12. List additional ideas

a. _____

b. _____

Using Testimonials Strategically

1. Choose the most powerful piece of the testimonial

What is the most convincing aspect of the testimonial? Is it the author? Where they are from? A specific sentence or paragraph they wrote? Be strategic about the aspect of the testimonial that you feature, and select what will have the most impact.

For example, you can compile a list titled *What Customers Are Saying* and list only the phrases that support your specific marketing message. Or you can feature the unique credentials or story of your customer before you even include their testimonial.

2. Put them on your website

Adding a page of testimonials to your website is a great start, especially when you're beginning to solicit customer responses. However, the most powerful way to ensure site visitors actually see your testimonials is to include them on every page – especially the ones with the highest traffic.

A testimonial should be placed wherever you make a strong statement about your service or product, and wherever the service or product is described. This is a great way to break up your sales copy with some "proof." As they read about your offering, your credibility will be validated by someone other than you.

3. Compile your best 25 to 50 letters in a display book

Like a proud grandparent, keep a book of testimonials in the waiting area of your office, your boardroom, and in your desk. Or put one at the service counter, cash register, and anywhere else people may have a moment to flip through.

I've seen this done in a recruiting firm, a hardware store, and a physiotherapist's office. When clients have a chance to read the positive experiences of others, they will be more open to hearing your sales pitch and be less guarded when responding to your unique offering.

With social media, you can create an electronic image on Facebook or Pinterest, and link to the images via LinkedIn or Twitter.

4. Hang your favorite testimonials in your store or office

Testimonials as art! Frame your favorite testimonials – preferably the ones written on client letterhead – and post them on the wall in your business. Even if clients don't read them up close, the volume and visual recognition of client logos will have impact. Plus – your next satisfied clients will want to see their company names on the wall, too.

5. Put them in your advertisements

Use short, clear, concise testimonials in your advertising. When was the last time you saw a prescription drug advertisement without a testimonial? Can't remember? That's because you haven't. The best advertisers know that testimonials are the fastest and most effective way to overcome skepticism and get clients thinking that your product or service is the solution to their problem.

6. Include a page of testimonials in your direct mail

When sending your marketing materials directly to a mass list of potential clients, let the words of others speak to the merits of your product or service. Put together a page or two of testimonials, and attach it to your mailing. The credibility of your company will be instantly established, encouraging clients to act – and buy – faster.

7. Partner with an associate for joint mailing

If you have an associate or colleague who has a similar customer base of new prospects for your business, try a joint-endorsed mailing. Each of you will send a letter to your own clients, endorsing the other's products and services. Your service or solution is offered to a potential client by a trusted source, and you are offering your existing clients the added value of an associated service to complement your own.

8. Leverage social media

If you are using social media (Facebook, LinkedIn, Google+, Twitter, Yelp, etc.) your electronic testimonials, may influence your customers and potential customers, (especially if they are already part of the social media communities where testimonials are posted about your product or services),

9. List additional ideas

a. _____

b. _____

c. _____

d. _____

Example: Testimonial Request Letter

Ms. Betty Smith, CEO
Small Business Company
123 Main Street
Philadelphia, PA 19103

December 15, 2012

Dear Ms. Smith,

Thank you for being a member of the Significant Business Results Gold-Level Coaching program. It was a pleasure helping you double your 2012 sales. Your preparation, commitment and follow-up made the coaching process work. more effective. We love being a trusted advisor because it means working with CEOs and entrepreneurial clients like yourself.

We know that you have choices when it comes to seeking business support, so thank you for choosing Significant Business Results LLC, www.SignificantBusinessResults.com.

We ask select customers for their feedback in the form of a testimonial. The real life experiences of our customers are stories that we are proud of, so we often use our customers' quotes in our marketing materials – specifically our website and sales brochures.

Will you to write down some of your feedback? A few words about your experience with the coaching process, and how we helped you double your sales? Please feel free to post your recommendation on LinkedIn.

Thank you in advance for your assistance.

Kind regards,

Franne McNeal, MBA
CEO

Example: Testimonial Thank You Letter

Ms. Betty Smith, CEO
Small Business Company
123 Main Street
Philadelphia, PA 19103

December 27, 2012

Dear Ms. Smith,

We received your glowing testimonial on LinkedIn and I wanted to thank you personally for your recommendation. Your return on investment from our Significant Business Results Gold-Level Coaching program is important to us.

We are thrilled that your business is growing beyond your expectations (doubled sales, reduction in expenses, more profits, higher lead conversation and increase client retention)!

When you enrolled in the 12-month Significant Business Results Gold-Level Coaching, we truly believed it would provide the continuing value for your business growth goals.

Thank you again for renewing your Significant Business Results Gold-Level Coaching membership for 2013.

We are all proud to have been of service to you and your company and look forward to seeing you in 2013.

Happy holidays and a prosperous new year.

Kind regards,

Franne McNeal, MBA
CEO

Testimonial Examples

Below are testimonials from online LinkedIn recommendations. Each testimonial is summarized with a headline.

Success and Profitability!

"Franne's knowledge and expertise are first rate. I sincerely appreciate her honesty and integrity. She is a great listener and is able to take the information I gave her, digest it quickly, guide me in the right direction and offer me alternative solutions that have led me to success and profitability in my event planning business. Franne is so inspiring and a genius in business strategy. She always has a new and fresh perspective when you think you've exhausted all your options. Her support and advice have been invaluable to me." Tammy Golson

Patience, Wisdom, Clarity!

"Franne had the uncanny ability to step inside my entrepreneurial mind, formulate the questions I wanted to ask but couldn't articulate, then proceed to answer those questions--with a patience, wisdom, and clarity I've not experienced anywhere else." Jeanine Caunt

Valuable Feedback!

"Franne provided valuable feedback and advice for my startup business. Her insights to refine the target market and focus the short-term strategy, immediately made a positive impact." Murray Jones

Brilliant. Dynamic. Accessible!

"I knew I need help getting my team behind the big growth plans I had in mind for 2013, but didn't know how to get there. Franne diagnosed and prescribed not just the right program, but the mental attitude and motivation that had to be at the heart of the roll out in order for it to work. Those insights yield 10x the outcome that I was expecting including new hiring procedures, new product offerings and a renewed determination that inspired me as a CEO. I'm grateful, and you will be too. I recommend Franne McNeal without one ounce of hesitation. Her insights are priceless and take home value, for us, was immediate." Susan Lindner

Whole New Level!

"Franne's ability is unparalleled. She quickly targeted where my business could improve and directed me in a way to help me take my private practice to a whole new level. I highly recommend her to anyone who wants to make a leap forward in their business." Will LeVasseur

Useful, Actionable Steps!

"Franne consistently provides honest, practical and valuable business advice. After all of our sessions, I have a clearer sense of direction and with useful, actionable steps to move my business forward. Franne is precise, efficient and shares deep insight into the key issues facing new entrepreneurs and seasoned investors." Joshua Wortman

Testimonial Worksheet

     Start today! Brainstorm a list of recent customers and clients who you will approach for testimonials. Post this worksheet in a visible place, and track your progress. Aim for fifty testimonials in two months. You can never have too many.

Name Phone	Request Letter Sent	Follow Up Call Made	Testimonial Received	Thank-you Letter Sent
	☐	☐	☐	☐
	☐	☐	☐	☐
	☐	☐	☐	☐
	☐	☐	☐	☐
	☐	☐	☐	☐
	☐	☐	☐	☐
	☐	☐	☐	☐
	☐	☐	☐	☐
	☐	☐	☐	☐
	☐	☐	☐	☐

Action Questions from Chapter 3

A. Current Testimonials

When and where do you get most of your testimonials?

Who gives you most of your testimonials?

B. Getting Testimonials

Which of the 11 strategies will help you get more testimonials?

C. Strategic Use of Testimonials

What is the most strategic use of your testimonials?

D. Testimonials Examples

Do you have three testimonials for each type of ideal client?

E. Testimonial Worksheet

Have you created a tracking process for your testimonials?

F. Next Step

What "doable" next step will facilitate significant business results?

4

Generate Unlimited Leads

Where Do Your Customers Come From?

Most people probably say: advertising, referrals or direct mail campaigns. This may seem true, but it's not really accurate.

Your customers come from leads that have been turned into sales. Each customer goes through a two-step process before they arrive with their wallets open. They have been converted from a member of a target market, to a lead, then to a customer.

When you advertise or send any marketing material out to your target market, you're not really trying to generate customers, you're trying to generate leads.

When you look at your marketing campaign from this perspective, the idea of generating leads as compared to customers seems easier. The pressure of closing sales is no longer placed on advertisements or brochures. From this perspective, the general purpose of your advertising and marketing efforts is to generate leads from qualified customers. Seems easy enough, doesn't it?

Where Are Your Leads Coming From?

If I asked you to tell me the top three ways you generate new sales leads, would you say?

- Advertising?
- Word of mouth?
- Networking?
- Don't know?

The first step toward increasing your leads is in understanding how many leads you currently get on a regular basis, as well as where they come from. Otherwise, how will you know when you're getting more phone calls or walk-in customers?

If you don't know where your leads come from, start *today*. Start asking every customer that comes through your door, "how did you hear about us?" or "what brought you in today?" Ask every customer that calls where they found your telephone number, or email address. Then *record the information for at least an entire week.*

When you're finished, take a look at your notes and write your top three lead generators.

1. _____
2. _____
3._____

From Lead to Customer: Conversion Rates

Leads mean nothing to your business unless you convert them into customers. You can get hundreds of leads from a single advertisement, but unless those leads result in purchases, it's been a largely unsuccessful (and costly) campaign.

The ratio of leads (potential customers) to transactions (actual customers) is called your conversion rate. Simply divide the number of customers who actually purchased something by the number of customers who inquired about your product or service, and multiply by 100.

 # transactions / # leads x 100 = % conversion rate

If, in a given week, you have 879 customers come into your store, and 143 of them purchase something, the formula would look like this:

[143 (customers) / 879 (leads)] x 100 = 16.25% conversion rate

What's Your Conversion Rate?

Based on the formula above, you can see that the higher your conversion rate, the more profitable your business.

Your next step is to determine you own current conversion rate. Add up the number of leads you sourced in the last section and divide that number into the total transactions that took place in the same week.

What is your conversion rate? Write it below:

_____

Quality and Qualified Leads

Based on our review of conversion rates, we can see that the number of leads you generate means nothing unless those leads are being converted into customers.

So what affects your ability (and the ability of your team) to turn leads into customers? Do you need to improve your scripts? Your product or service? Find a more competitive edge in the marketplace?

Maybe, but the first step toward increasing conversion rates is to evaluate the leads you are currently generating and make sure those leads are the right ones.

What are Quality Leads?

Potential customers are potential customers, right? Anyone who walks into your store or picks up the phone to call your business can be convinced to purchase from you, right? Not necessarily, but this is a common assumption most business owners make.

Quality leads are the people who are the most likely to buy your product or service. They are the qualified buyers who comprise your target market. Anyone might walk in off the street to browse a furniture store – regardless of whether or not they are in the market for a new couch or bed frame. This lead is solely interested in browsing, and is not likely to be converted to a customer.

A quality lead is someone looking for a new kitchen table, and who specifically drove to that same furniture store because a friend had raved about the service they received that month. These are the kinds of leads you need to focus on generating.

How Do You Get Quality Leads?

1. Know your target market

Get a handle on who your customers are – the people who are most likely to buy your product or service. Know their age, sex, income, and purchase motivations. From that information, you can determine how best to reach your specific audience.

2. Focus on the 80/20 rule

A common statistic in business is that 80% of your revenue comes from 20% of your customers. These are your star clients, or your ideal clients. These are the clients you should focus your efforts on recruiting. This is the easiest way to grow your business and your income.

3. Get specific

Focus not only on who you want to attract, but how you're going to attract them. If you're trying to generate leads from a specific market segment, craft a unique offer to get their attention.

4. Be proactive

Once you've generated a slew of leads, make sure you have the resources to follow-up on them. Be diligent and aggressive, and follow-up in a timely manner. You've done work to get them, now reel them in.

Get More Leads from Existing Strategies

Increasing your lead generation doesn't necessarily mean diving in and implementing an expensive array of new marketing strategies. Marketing and customer outreach for the purpose of lead generation can be inexpensive and bring a high return on investment.

You are likely already implementing many of these strategies. With a little tweaking or refinement, you can easily double your leads and ensure they are more qualified. Here are some popular ways to generate quality leads:

1.   Direct mail to your ideal customers

Direct mail is one of the fastest and most effective ways to generate leads that will build your business. It's a simple strategy – in fact, you're probably already reaching out to potential clients through direct mail letters with enticing offers.

The secret to doubling your results is to craft your direct mail campaigns specifically to a highly targeted audience of your *ideal* customers.

Your ideal customers are the people who will buy the most of your products or services. They are the customers who will buy from you over and over again, and refer your business to their friends. They are the 20% of your clients who make up 80% of your revenue.

2.   Identify your ideal customers

Who are your ideal customers? What is their age, sex, income, location, and purchase motivation? Where do they live? How do they spend their money? Be as specific as possible.

Once you have identified who your ideal customers are, you can begin to determine how you can go about reaching them. Will you mail to households or apartment buildings? Families or retirees? Direct mail lists are available for purchase from a wide range of companies, and can be segregated into a variety of demographic and socio-graphic categories.

3. Craft a special offer

Create an offer that's too good to refuse – not for your entire target market, but for your ideal customer. How can you cater to their unique needs and wants? What will be irresistible for them?

For example, if you operate a furniture store, your target market is a broad range of people. However, if you are targeting young families, your offer will be much different than one you may craft for empty-nesters.

4. Court them for their business

Don't stop at a single mail-out. Sometimes people will throw your letter away two or three times before they are motivated to act. Treat your direct mail campaign like a courtship, and understand that it will happen over time.

First send a letter introducing yourself and your irresistible offer. Then follow-up on a monthly basis with additional letters, newsletters, offers, or flyers. Repetition and reinforcement of your presence is how your customer will go from saying, "who is this company" to "I buy from this company."

Most individuals will need at least nine to twelve exposures to you and your message before your message is recognizable and relevant.

Advertise for Lead Generation

Statistics show that nearly 50% of all purchase decisions are motivated by advertising. It can also be a relatively cost effective way of generating leads.

We've already discussed the importance of ensuring your advertisements are purpose-focused. The general purpose of most advertisements is to increase sales – which starts with leads. Some ads are created solely for lead generation – to get the customers to pick up the phone or walk in the store.

Lead generation ads have a simple design and create a sense of curiosity or mystery. Often, they feature an almost unbelievable offer. Their purpose is not to convince the customer to buy, but to contact the business for more information.

As always, when you are targeting your ideal audience, you'll need to ensure that your ads are placed prominently in publications that your audience reads. This doesn't mean that you have to fork over the cash for expensive display ads. Inexpensive advertising in e-mail newsletters, classifieds, and the yellow pages are very effective for lead generation.

Tips for Lead Generation Advertising

1. Leverage low-cost advertising

Place ads in e-mail, newsletters, Facebook and Google Adwords, as well as the classified sections of publications.

2. Spark curiosity

Don't give them all the information they need to make a decision. Ask them to contact you for the full story or the complete details of the seemingly outrageous offer.

3. Grab them with a killer headline

Like all advertising, a compelling headline is essential. Focus on the greatest benefits to the customer, or feature an unbelievable offer. Effective killer headlines are three to eight words. There are many resources for identifying "words that sell", evoke emotion and action. A marketing, copywriting, and/or branding professional can assist you. Also look at what is effective both within and outside of your industry.

4. Referrals and strategic relationships

A referral system is one of the most profitable systems you can create in your business. The beauty is that once it's set up, it often runs itself.

Customers that come to you through referrals are often your "ideal customers." They are already trusting and willing to buy. This is one of the most cost-effective methods of generating new business, and is often the most profitable. These referral clients will buy more, faster, and refer further business to your company.

Referrals naturally happen without much effort for reputable businesses, but with a proactive referral strategy, you'll certainly double or triple your referrals. Sometimes you just need to ask!

Easy Referral Strategies to Implement

1. Referral incentives

Give your customers a reason to refer business to you. Reward them with discounts, gifts, or free service in exchange for a successful referral.

2. Referral program

Offer new customers a free product or service to get them in the door. Then at the end of the transaction, give them three more "coupons" for the same free product or service that they can give to their friends. Do the same with their friends. This ongoing program will bring you more business than you can imagine.

3. Strategic relationships

Forge alliances with non-competitive companies who target your ideal customers. Create cross-promotion and cross-referral email campaigns that benefit both businesses.

Lead Management Systems

Once your lead generation strategies are in place, you'll also need a system to manage incoming inquiries. You'll need to ensure that you receive enough information from each lead to follow-up on at a later date. You'll also need to create a system to organize that information, and track the lead as it is converted into a sale.

Gathering Information from Your Leads

Here is a list of information that you should gather from your leads. This list can be customized to the needs of your business, and the type of information you can realistically ask for from your potential customers.

- Company Name
- Name of Contact
- Alternate Contact Person
- Mailing Address
- Phone Number
- Fax Number
- Cell Phone

- Email Address
- Website Address
- Product/Service of Interest
- Other Competitors

Lead List Management Methods

Once you have gathered information from your lead, you'll need a system to organize their information and keep a detailed contact history.

The simplest way to do this is with a database program, but you can also use a variety of hard copy methods.

1. **Electronic database programs**

   - High level of organization available
   - Unlimited space for notes and record-keeping
   - Data-entry required
   - Examples include: MS Access, Customer Relationship Management (CRM) Software

2. **Index cards**

   - Variety of sizes: 3x5, 4x6 or 5x8
   - Basic contact information on one side
   - Notes on the other side

3. Notebook

- Best if leads are managed by a single person
- Lots of room for notes
- Inexpensive
- Difficult to re-organize
- Best for smaller lists

5. Business Card Organizer

- Best for small lists – under 100
- Limited space for notes
- No data entry required
- Rolodex-style, or clear binder pages

6. List additional ideas

- _____
- _____
- _____
- _____
- _____
- _____
- _____
- _____
- _____
- _____

Action Questions from Chapter 4

A. Your Leads

Where do you get your leads?

B. Your Conversion Rate

What is your current conversion rate?

What is your desired conversion rate?

C. Quality Leads

What currently is a quality lead for you?

What is your desired quality lead?

D. Getting Quality Leads

What is your target market?

How are your focusing on the 80/20 rule?

How are you going to attract specific leads?

What is your follow-up process?

E. Existing Strategies

What are your existing strategies for quality leads?

Action Questions from Chapter 4, continued

F. Qualifying Leads

What do you do to qualify your leads?

G. Lead Generating Ad Strategies

Which lead generating ad strategies will be most effective for you?
- Leverage low cost advertising
- Spark curiosity
- Grab them with a killer headline
- Referrals and strategic relationships

H. Referral Strategies

Which referral strategies will you implement?

I. Lead Management System

How will you set up your lead management system?
What lead list management methods will you implement?

J. Next Step

What "doable" next step will facilitate significant business results?

5

Create Immediate Sales

You Are In Sales

If you're a business owner, you're also a salesperson.

You've had to sell the bank to get them to loan you your start-up capital. You've had to sell the best employees on why they should work for your business. You've had to convince your business partner, spouse, and friends why your business idea is a good one.

Now you have to repeatedly sell your product or service to your customers.

The ability to sell effectively and efficiently is one every successful business owner has cultivated, and continues to develop. It can be a complicated and time consuming task; one that you will have to continually work on throughout your career in order to be – and stay – successful.

Fortunately, making sales is a step-by-step process that can be learned, customized, and continuously improved. There are a wide range of tools available to help and support your sales efforts.

You don't have to be the most outgoing, enthusiastic person to be successful at sales. You don't even have to be a good public speaker. All you need is an understanding of the basic sales process and a genuine passion for what you are selling.

Sales 101

The sales process varies according to the type of business, type of customers, and type of product or service that is offered; however, the core steps are the same. Similarly, sales training varies from individual to individual, but the core skills and abilities remain the same.

Making sales is a process. There are clear, step-by-step actions that can be taken and that result in a sale.

Here is a basic seven-step process that you can follow or fine tune to suit your unique products and services. Remember that each step is important and builds on the step previous. It is essential to become adept at each step, instead of focusing on closing the sale.

As part of your clarifying your competitive advantage, evaluate how your competitor's handle each of the following steps.

1. Preparation

Make sure you have prepared for your meeting or presentation. You have complete control of this part of the sales process, so it is important to do everything you can to set the stage for your success.

- Understand your product or service inside and out.
- Prepare all the necessary materials and organize them neatly.
- Keep your place of business tidy and organized. Reface products on shelves.
- Ensure you appear professional and well groomed.
- Do some research on your potential client and brainstorm to find common ground.

2. Build a relationship

The first few minutes that you spend with a potential customer set the stage for the rest of your interaction. First impressions are everything. Your goal in the second step is to relax the customer and begin to develop a relationship with them. Establishing a real relationship with your customer creates trust.

- Make a great first impression
- Shake hands, make eye contact, and introduce yourself.
- Remain confident and professional, but also personable.
- Mirror their speech and behavior.
- Begin with general questions and small talk.

- Show interest in them and their place of business.
- Notice and comment on positives.
- Find some common ground on which to relate.

3. Discuss needs + wants

Once you have spent a few moments getting to know your prospect, start asking open-ended questions to discover some of their needs and wants.

- In retail: Ask what brought them in the store.
- In a meeting: Ask why they are interested in or what criteria they have in mind for that product or service.
- In a sales presentation: Ask for a few moments at the outset to outline the purpose of your visit, as well as how you have structured the presentation.
- Listen intently and repeat back information that you are not sure you understood.
- Ask open-ended questions to get them talking. The longer they talk, the more insight they are providing you into their needs and purchase motivations.
- Ask clarifying questions about their responses.
- If you become sure the customer is going to buy your product or service, begin asking questions specific to the offering. For example, what size/color do you prefer?

4. Present the solution

Once you have a solid understanding of what they are looking for, or what issue they are looking to resolve, you can begin to present the solution: your product or service.

- Explain how your product or service solves their problem or meeting their needs. If several products apply, begin by presenting the mid-level product.
- Illustrate your points with anecdotes about other happy customers, or awards the product or service has earned.
- Use hypothetical examples featuring your customer. Encourage them to picture a scenario after their purchase.
- Begin by describing the benefits of the product, then follow-up with features and advantages.
- Watch your customer's behavior as you speak and ask further qualifying questions based on their body language and tone.
- Give the customer an opportunity to ask you questions or provide feedback about each product or service after you have described it.
- Ask closed-ended questions to gain agreement.

5. Overcome objections

As you present the product or service, take note of potential objections by asking open-ended questions and monitoring body language. Expect that objections will arise and prepare for them. Consider brainstorming a list of all potential objections and writing down your responses.

- Repeat the objection back to the customer to ensure you understand them correctly.
- Empathize with what they have said and then provide a response that overcomes the objection.
- Confirm that the answer you have provided has overcome their objection by repeating yourself.

The Eight Most Common Objections

1. The product or service does not seem valuable to me.
2. There is no reason for me to act know. I will wait.
3. It's safest not to make a decision right away.
4. There is not enough money for the purchase.
5. The competitor offers a better product.
6. There are internal issues between people/departments.
7. The relationship with the decision maker is strained.
8. There is an existing contract in place with another business.

---

6. Close

This is an important part of the sales process that should be handled delicately. Deciding when to close is a judgment call that must be made in the moment, during the sale. Ideally, you have presented a solution to their problem, have overcome objections, and have the customer in a place where they are ready to buy.

Here are some questions to ask before you close the sale:

- Does my prospect agree that there is value in my product or service?
- Does my prospect understand the features and benefits of the product or service?
- Are there any remaining objections that must be handled?
- What other factors can influence my prospect's decision to buy?
- Have I minimized the risk involved in the purchase and provided some level of urgency for the purchase?

Once you have determined that it is time to make the sale, here are some sample statements that you can use to get the process rolling:

- So should we get started?
- Shall I grab a new one from the back?
- If you just give me your credit card, I can take care of the transaction while you continue browsing.
- When do you want the product delivered?
- We can begin next month when we receive payment on the 15th.
- May I email you a draft contract tomorrow?

7.   Service + follow-up

Once you have made the sale, your work is not over. You want to ensure that the customer will become a loyal, repeat customer and that they will refer their friends to your business.

Ask them to be in your customer database and keep in touch with regular newsletters. Follow-up with a phone call or drop by to ask how they are enjoying the product or service, and if they have any further questions or needs you can assist them with.

This contact opportunity also allows you to ask for a referral or an up sell. At the very least, it will ensure you are continuing to foster and build a relationship with the client.

Up-Selling

Up-selling is simply inviting your customers to spend more money in your business by purchasing additional products or services. This can include more of the same product, complementary products, or impulse items.

Regardless, up-selling is an effective way to increase profits and create loyal clients – without spending any money to acquire the business. These clients are already purchasing from you – which means they perceive value in what you have to offer – so take the information that you have gained in the sales process and offer them a little bit more.

You experience up-selling on a daily basis. Examples include: "do you want fries with that?" to "have you heard about our product protection program?" Companies across the globe have tapped into and trained their team on the value of the up-sell.

Up-selling is truly rooted in good customer service. If your client purchases a new computer printer, you'll need to make sure that they have the cords required to connect it to the computer, regular and photo paper, and color and black & white ink.

If you don't suggest these items, they may arrive home and realize that they do not have all the materials needed to use the product. They may choose to purchase those materials somewhere closer, cheaper, or more helpful.

Customer education is another form of up-selling. What if your customer doesn't realize that you sell a variety of printer paper and stationery, in addition to computer hardware like printers? Take every opportunity to educate your customer on the products and services that you offer that may be of interest to them.

An effective way of implementing an up-sell system into your business is simply by creating add-on checklists for the products or services you offer. Each item has a list of related items that your customer may need. This will encourage your team to develop the habit of asking for the up-sell.

Other up-sell strategies can be implemented:

1. **At the point of sale.** This is a great place for impulse items like candy and flashlights, etc.

2. **In a newsletter.** This is an effective strategy for customer education.

3. **In your merchandising.** Place strips of impulse items near related items. For example, paper clips with paper and pens near binders.

4. **Over the phone.** If someone is placing an order for delivery, offer additional items in the same shipment for convenience.

5. **With new products.** Feature each new product or service that you offer prominently in your business, and ask your team to mention it to every customer.

6. **List additional ideas.**

    a. _____

    b. _____

    c. _____

    d. _____

What Makes a Good Salesperson?

There are a lot of salespeople out there – but what qualities and skills make a great salesperson?

These are the attributes you want to find or develop in your team:

- Willingness to continuously learn and improve sales skills.
- Sincerity in relating to customers
- Commitment to providing solutions to customer objectives
- An understanding of the company's big picture
- A communication style that is direct, polite, and professional
- Honesty and respect for other team members and customers
- Ability to manage time
- Enthusiastic
- Inquisitive
- A great listener
- Ability to quickly interpret, analyze, and respond during the sale
- Ability to connect and develop relationships of trust
- Professional appearance

Team Building: Keeping Your Team Together

In many businesses, sales is a department or a whole team of people who work together to generate leads and convert customers. Effective management of your sales team is a skill every business owner should cultivate.

Important aspects of managing a sales team

1. Communication

- Targets and results regularly reviewed
- Opportunities for input regularly provided
- Sales team members have a clear understanding of what is expected
- All team members know daily, weekly, and quarterly targets
- Having an electronic system of tracking communication
- Technology and information security policy

2. Performance management

- Sales team members motivated to reach targets
- Sales team recognized and rewarded once those targets are reached
- Opportunities for skills training and development
- Team has broad and comprehensive product and industry knowledge
- Opportunity for growth within the company
- Performance regularly reviewed

3. Operations

- Solid understanding of numbers (revenue, profit, margins)

- Sales processes regularly reviewed
- Variety of sales scripts prepared
- Measure conversion rates
- Know how sales leads are generated

4. List additional ideas

- _____
- _____

Virtual Team Building: Leveraging Technology

How are you using smart phones, video, text, etc. to keep in touch with your sales team? What is your team's preferred method of communication?

Are you using any of the following?

1. Teleseminars
2. Webinars
3. Online video
4. Phone based video

Sales Tools

Every salesperson should have an arsenal of tools on hand to assist them in the sales process. These tools can act as aids while a sale is taking place, or help to foster continual learning and development of the salesperson's skills and approach.

Popular Sales Tools

Tool	Description + Benefit
Scripts	Used for incoming and outgoing telemarketing, cold calls, door-to-door sales, in-store sales. Create several different scripts for your business. Maintain consistency in your sales approach. Revise and renew your scripts regularly.
Presentation Materials	High-quality information about your product or service. Forms, PowerPoint, brochures, product sheets and proposals outline your presentations.
Colleagues	A source of help and advice, especially when you are on the same team or sell similar products. Also a source of support.
Customer Databases	An accurate, up-to-date database of customer contact information and contact history. Used to stay in touch with clients. Can also be used for direct mail and follow-up telemarketing.

The Internet	A powerful resource for sales help and advice. Information to help improve your sales process. Online sales coaching. Source for product knowledge.
Ongoing Training	Constant improvement of your sales skills. Constant increase in product knowledge. Investment in yourself and your company.
List Additional Ideas	

8 Tips for Better Sales

1. Dress for the sale

Dress professionally, appear well put together, and maintain good hygiene. Ensure that you are not only dressed professionally, but *appropriately*.

Will your client feel more comfortable if you wore a suit, or jeans and blazer?

2. Speak their language

Show you understand their industry or culture and use phrases your ustomer understands. This may require researching industry jargon or common phrases. Remember to avoid using words and phrases that are used in the sales process: sold, contract, telemarketing, finance, interest, etc. Doing so will help break down the salesperson vs. customer barrier.

3. Ooze positivity

Show up or answer the phone with a smile, and leave your personal or business issues behind. Be enthusiastic about what you have to offer and how that offering will benefit your customer. Reflect this not only in your voice, but also in your body language.

4. Deliver a strong pitch or presentation

Be confident and convincing. Leave self-doubt at the door, and walk in assuming the sale. Take time to explain complex concepts, and always connect what you're saying to your audience in a specific way.

5. Be a poster-child for good manners

Listen intently, don't interrupt, don't show up late, have a strong handshake, and give everyone you are speaking to equal attention. Be aware of cultural preferences regarding gift giving and tokens of appreciation.

6. Avoid sensitive subjects

Politics, religion, swearing, sexual innuendos, and racial comments are absolutely off-limits. So are negative comments about other customers or the competition.

7. Create a real relationship

Icebreakers and small talk are not just to pass the time before your presentation. They are how relationships get established. Show genuine interest in everything your customer has to say. Ask questions about topics you know they are passionate about. Speak person to person, not salesperson to customer. Remember everything.

8. Know more than you need to

Impress clients with comprehensive knowledge – not only of your product or service, but also of the people who use that product or service, and industry trends. Focus on being seen as an expert in order to build trust and respect.

9. List additional ideas

a. _____

b. _____

c. _____

Action Questions from Chapter 5

A. 7-Step Sales Process

What will you do to "prepare"?

What will you say to "build a relationship"?

What will you say to "discuss needs and wants"?

What will you say to "present the solution"?

What will you say to "overcome objections"?

What will you say to "close"?

What will you do to "service + follow-up"?

B. Up-selling

What will be part of your up-sell process?

Which up-sell strategies will you implement?

C. Sales Team

How will you build your sales team?

How will you leverage sales tools?

How will you leverage technology?

Which of the 8 tips for better sales will you implement?

D. Next Step

What "doable" next step will facilitate significant business results?

6

Use Scripts to Increase Sales

Script Are Guides

What do playbooks, prompts, guides, and scripts all have in common?

They are all popular tools that dictate or guide human behavior toward a desired outcome.

Playbooks help coaches tell sports teams specifically how to play the game to overcome an opponent. Prompts help to kick-start writers and other creative professionals when stuck in a rut. Guides provide a series of instructions so that a person or team of people can complete or implement a specific task. Film scripts tell actors how to act for a particular part.

If you're in the business of sales, sales scripts are tools that guide salespeople during interactions or conversations with potential customers.

A large number of businesses use scripts, either as a way of maintaining consistency among a sales team, training new salespeople, or enhancing their sales skills. They may have a single script or several, and may change their scripts regularly or use the same one for years.

What most businesses overlook, however, is that the sales script is a living, breathing, changing member of their sales team. They may be internal documents, but they deserve just as much time and effort as your marketing collateral.

Do You Really Need a Script?

The short answer is yes. You absolutely need a script for any and every customer interaction that you and your salespeople may find yourselves in.

Sure, countless business owners and salespeople work every day without a script. If you own your own business, chances are you're already a pretty good salesperson. But if you are not using scripts, you're only working at half of your true potential – or getting half of your potential earnings.

Scripts don't have to be "cheesy" or read verbatim. They act as a map for your sales process and provide prompts to trigger your memory and keep you on track. How many times have you made a cold call that didn't work out the way you wanted? Scripts dramatically improve the effectiveness and efficiency of your sales processes.

A comprehensive set of scripts also keeps a level of consistency among your salespeople and the customer service they provide your clients.

Once scripts are written, memorized, and rehearsed, they become like film scripts; the salesperson can breathe their own life and personality into the conversation, while staying focused on the call's objectives.

Why Your Scripts Aren't Working

If you are currently using scripts in your business, are they working?

- Are they as effective as they could possibly be?
- How do you know?
- When was the last time they were reviewed or updated?

Scripts are like any other element of your marketing campaign – they need to be tested and measured for results, and changed based on what is or is not working.

Measure the success of your script based on your conversion rates. Of all the people you speak to using the script, how many are being converted from leads to sales? Which scripts are more effective in conversions? Do the seasonality or marketing promotions impact conversions?

When evaluating your existing scripts, ask the following questions:

1. How old is this script?

2. What was it written for?

Scripts are living, breathing members of your company. They need to be written and rewritten again as the needs of your customers change, your product or services change, or as new strategies are implemented.

a. Does this script address all the customer objections?

Every time you hear a customer raise an objection that is not included on the script, add the good answer that worked for you into the script. The power of your script lies in the ability to anticipate customer concerns and answer them before they're raised.

b. Does this script sound the same as the others?

Your scripts are part of the package that represents you as a company. There should be a consistent feel or approach throughout your scripts that your customers will recognize and feel confident in dealing with.

c. Is everyone using the script?

Who on your team regularly uses these scripts? Just the junior team? Only the top-performing team? Make sure everyone is singing from the same song sheet – your customers will appreciate the consistency.

Types of Scripts

Depending on the product or service that you offer and the marketing strategies that you have chosen, there are countless types of scripts that you can potentially prepare for your business,

When you sit down to create your scripts, it is wise to start by making a list of all the instances that you and your team members interact with your existing or potential customers. Then prioritize the list from most to least important, and start writing from the top.

Here are some commonly used scripts and their purposes:

1. Sales presentation script

Each time you or your sales team make a presentation, they should be using the same or a slightly modified version of the same script. This script includes sample icebreakers, a presentation on benefits and features of the product or service, and a list of possible objections and responses. These scripts should also help alleviate some of the nervousness or anxiety associated with public speaking.

This could include your 15-second, 3-second, and 1-minute introduction or elevator speech which use during networking events. However, remember that introductions or elevator speeches need to be tailored to the listener, while maintaining consistent core elements.

2. Closing script

Closing scripts help you do just that: close the sale. This can include a list of closing prompts or statements to get the transaction started. This type of script also includes a list of possible customer objections and planned responses.

3. Incoming phone call script

Everyone who calls your business should be treated the same way; consistent information should be gathered and provided to the customer. The person answering the phone should state the company name, department name, and their own name in the initial greeting. This goes for both the main line, and each individual or department extension.

Your voicemail and any message related to your phone system is important. How are you using your cell phone and online phone services that automatically go to voicemail, or automatically connect to your cell phone?

4. Cold call script

This is one of the most important scripts that you can perfect for your business. The cold call script must master the art of quickly getting the attention of the customer, then engaging and persuading them with the benefits of the product or service. The caller needs to establish common ground with the potential customer and find a way to get them talking through open-ended questions.

5. Direct mail follow-up script

Scripts for outgoing calls that are intended to follow-up on a direct mail piece are essential for every direct mail campaign. They are designed 2to call qualified leads that have already received information and an offer, and convert them into customers. These scripts should focus on enticing customers to act and overcoming any objections that may have prevented them from acting sooner.

6. Market research script

Scripts that are used primarily for the purpose of gathering information should be designed to get the customer talking. A focus on open-ended questions and relationship building statements helps to relax the customer and encourages honest dialogue.

7. Difficult customer script

Just like every salesperson needs to practice the sales process, you and your team also need to practice your ability to handle difficult customers. If you operate a retail business, then this is especially important, as difficult customers often present themselves in front of other customers. These scripts should help you diffuse the situation, calm the customer, and then handle their objections.

8. Creating scripts

Creating powerful scripts is not a complicated exercise, but it will take some time to complete. Focus on the most vital scripts for your business first, and engage the assistance of your sales team in drafting or reviewing the scripts.

Your Script Binder

Keep master copies of all of your scripts in one organized place. An effective way to do this is to create a binder and use tabs to separate each type of script.

You also want to create a separate tab for customer objections, and list every single customer objection you have ever heard in relation to your product or service. Find a way to organize each objection so you can easily find them – group them by category or separate them with tabs.

Then list your responses next to each objection – there should be several responses to each objection created with different customer types in mind. A master list of customer objections and responses is an invaluable tool for any business owner, salesperson, and script writer. The more responses you can think of, the better.

Remember, the script binder is never "finished." You will need to make sure that it is updated and added to on a regular basis. At the beginning of each quarter, identify one-hour time slots each month for your team to update their written scripts and test the script in a role-play situation.

Writing Scripts – Step by Step

Step One: Record What You're Doing Now

If you aren't using scripts – or even if you are – start by recording yourself in action. Use video or audio recording to tape yourself on the phone, in a sales presentation, or with a customer.

Make notes on your body language, word choice, customer reaction and body language, responses to objections, and closing statements. You may also wish to ask an associate to make notes on your performance and discuss them with you in a constructive fashion.

Step Two: Evaluate What You're Doing Wrong

Take a look at your notes, and ask yourself the following questions:

- How are you engaging the customer?
- Are you building common ground and trust?
- Does what you are saying matter to the customer?
- Is your offer a powerful one?
- What objections are raised?
- How are you dealing with them?
- What objections are you avoiding?
- How natural is your close?
- Are you as effective as you think you can be?

Once you have answered and made notes in response to these questions, make a list of things that you need to improve, and how you think you might go about doing so. Do you need to strengthen your closing statements? Do you need to brainstorm more responses to objections? Remember that everyone's script and sales process can be improved.

Step Three: Decide Who the Script is For

So now that you know the elements of your script you need to work on, you can begin drafting your new script or revising an old one.

The first part of writing a script – or any piece of marketing material – is having a strong understanding of who you are writing it for. Who is your target audience? What does your ideal customer look like? Consider demographic characteristics like age, sex, location, income, occupation, and marital status. Be as specific as possible. What are their purchase patterns? What motivates them to spend money?

If you are writing a cold call script, you need to develop or purchase a list of people who falls into the target market specifics you have established. If you are writing a sales script for in-store customers, then review what types of customers find their way into your place of business.

You want to use words that your target audience will not only understand, but relate to and resonate with.

Use sensory language that triggers emotional and feeling responses – I need this, this will solve that problem, I'll feel better if I have this, etc.

Step Four: Decide What You Want to Say

There are typically five sections of every script – and there may be more, depending on the type and purpose of script:

1. **Engage**

   - Get their attention or pique their interest.
   - Establish common ground.
   - Build trust, be human.
   - Ask for their time.

2. **Ask + qualify**

   - Take control of the conversation by asking questions.
   - Use open-ended questions that can't have a "yes" or "no."
   - Get the customer talking.
   - Ask as many questions as you need to get information on the customer's needs and purchase motivations.

3. **Get agreement**

   - Ask closed-ended questions that they will respond with "yes."
   - Get them to agree on the benefits of the product or service.
   - Repeat key points back to the customer to gain agreement.

4. Overcome objections

- Anticipate objections based on customer comments, then refute them.
- Make informative assumptions about their thought process, identify with their concern, then refute it using your own experiences.
- Repeat concerns back to the customer to let them know you have heard them.
- Ask about any remaining objections before you close.

5. Close

- Assume that you have overcome all objections, and have the sale.
- Ask the customer transactional questions, like delivery timing and payment method.
- Be as confident and natural as possible.

Step Five: Train Your Team

Once you have written your company's scripts, you need to ensure that your team understands and are comfortable using them.

Consider having a team meeting and use role playing to review each of the scripts. This will encourage your salespeople to practice among each other and strengthen their sales skills. Ask them for feedback on the scripts and make any necessary changes.

You also need to decide how comfortable you are having your salespeople personalizing the scripts to suit their own styles. Be clear on what elements of the script are "company standards" and essential techniques, but also be flexible with your team.

Step Six: Continually Revise

After you have carefully crafted your script, put it to the test. Practice on your colleagues, friends, and family. Get their feedback and make changes.

Remember that scripts need to change and evolve as your business changes and evolves and new products or services are introduced. Keep your script binder on your desk at all times and continually make changes and improvements to it.

You may also wish to record and evaluate your performance on a regular basis. This is an exercise that you could incorporate into regular employee reviews, to use as a constructive tool for team development.

Step Seven: List Additional Ideas

a.   _____

b.   _____

c.   _____

Script Tips

1. **Practice anticipating and eliciting real objections**, including the ones your customer doesn't want to raise.

2. **Make the script yours.** It should look, feel, and sound like you naturally do, not like you're reading off the page.

3. **Spend time with the masters.** If there is a salesperson that you admire in your community, ask to observe them in action. Take notes on their performance and the techniques they use for success.

4. **If your script is not successful, ask the customer why not?** Even if you don't get the sale, you'll get a new objection that you can craft responses to and never get stumped by it again.

5. **Don't fear objections.** Just spend time identifying as many as possible, then practice overcoming them.

6. **Never stop thinking of responses to customer objections.** Each objection could potentially have thirty responses geared toward specific customer types.

7. **Anecdotes are persuasive writing tools.** Use them in your scripts. People enjoy hearing stories, especially stories that relate to them and their experiences, frustrations, and troubles. Let the story sell your product or service for you.

8. **Include body language in your scripts.** It's just as important as your words. Try mimicking your subject's posture, arm position, and seating position. This is proven to create ease and build trust.

9. **If you only have your voice, use it**. Pay attention to tone, language choice, speed, and background noise. You only have sound to establish a trusting relationships, so do it carefully.

10. **Be confident.** Focus on a positive stream of self-talk to prepare for the call or presentation. Confidence sells.

11. **Spend time on your closing scripts.** They are a critical component of your presentation or phone call. This can be a challenging part of the sales process, so practice, practice, practice.

12. **List additional ideas**

   a. _____

   b. _____

   c. _____

   d. _____

   e. _____

Action Questions from Chapter 6

A. Your Current Scripts

What's working with your current scripts?

What's not working with your current scripts?

B. Scripts Needed

Which scripts would provide immediate results?
- Sales presentation, closing, incoming phone call
- Direct mail follow-up, email follow-up
- Market research, cold call
- Difficult customer

C. Script Content

What will you say to "engage"?

What will you say to "ask + qualify?

What will you say to "get agreement"?

What will you say to "overcome objections"?

What will you say to "close"?

D. Next Step

Which script tips will you implement?

What "doable" next step will facilitate significant business results?

7

Create Repeat Business

Existing Customers Are Valuable

When it comes to marketing and generating more income, most business owners are focused outward.

They've carefully established and segmented their target market, and created specific offers and messages for each market segment. They spend thousands of dollars in advertising and direct mail campaigns in hot pursuit of more leads, more customers, and more foot traffic.

While this is an effective way to build a business, it is costly and time consuming. It requires constant and consistent effort, and while this approach does generate results, those results quickly disappear when the effort stops or becomes less intense.

Successful businesses that see sustained growth have a double-edged marketing strategy. They focus their efforts *outward* – on new potential customers and marketing – as well as *inward* – on existing customers and referral business.

These successful businesses have leveraged their existing efforts to generate more revenue. Simply put, their customers buy from them over and over again.

For most businesses, this is the easiest way to increase their revenues. Simple customer loyalty strategies and outstanding customer service are often all you need to dramatically increase your sales – from the customers you already have. Think about how you can help your customers "pay, stay and refer".

The Cost of Your Customers

Do you know how much it costs your business to buy new customers?

Each new customer that walks through your door – with the exception of referrals – has cost you money to acquire. You have spent money on advertising and promotions to generate leads and turn those leads into customers.

For example, if you have placed an ad in your local newspaper for $1,000, and the ad brings in 10 customers, you have paid $100 to acquire

each customer. You would need to ensure each of those customers spent at least $200 to cover your margin and break even.
.

Alternately, if you spent two hours of your time and $10 per month on an email marketing program to send a newsletter to your existing database of customers, and you bring in 10 customers as a result – each customer has cost you $1.

Generating more repeat business means focusing on the marketing strategies that aim to keep your existing customers instead of purchase new ones – effectively reducing the cost of attracting new customers to your business.

These strategies are simple to implement and don't require much time investment, just a solid understanding of how to make customers want to come back and spend more of their money.

Keeping Your Customers

Marketing strategies that focus on keeping your current customer base are easy and enjoyable to implement. They allow you to build real relationships with the people you do business with, instead of dealing with a revolving door of people on the other end of your sales process.

Repeat customers create a community of people around your

business that presumably share the same needs, desires and frustrations. The information you gain from these customers (market research) can help you strengthen the understanding of your target audience and more accurately segment it. Repeat customers are often called "brand ambassadors" because they enthusiastically talk about the benefits of your products and services.

Remember – 80% of your revenue comes from 20% of your customers. Always focus on these customers. They are ideal customers that you want to recruit and hold on to.

1. Customer service: make them love buying from you

Every business, even those with excellent service standards, can improve the service they provide their customers. Customer service seems to be a dying concept in most businesses; more focus seems to be placed on the speed of the transaction. These days, you can even go to the grocery store now and not speak to a single sales associate thanks to self-serve checkouts.

To improve your company's customer service standards, take a survey of your customers and your employees to brainstorm ways you can improve the experience of buying from your business. Successful customer service standards that make your customers buy include:

    a. <u>Consistency</u>. The standards are written (online, in company manuals, discussed in meetings, shared in marketing materials, etc.), and used by every person in your organization.

Expectations are clear and followed through. Customers know what to expect and choose your business because of those expectations. This consistency is becomes part of your brand and the perception of your brand. Consistent customer service is a competitive business advantage that helps you command higher prices.

b. Convenience. It is nearly effortless for the customer to spend money at your place of business. Convenience can take many forms – location, product selection, value-added services like delivery – and it is also consistent.

c. Customer-driven. The service that the customer receives is exactly how they want to be treated when buying your product or service. It is reflective of your target market, and appropriate to their lifestyle. Customers will probably not appreciate white linen tablecloths at a fast food restaurant, but they do appreciate a two minutes or less guarantee.

2. Newsletters: keep in touch with your customers

A regular newsletter is an easy, time-effective, and inexpensive marketing strategy to implement. Unfortunately, many small businesses think these are too time consuming and too expensive to adopt as part of their marketing strategy.

The most popular type of newsletter distribution is email. This will cost your business as little at $10 per month for an email marketing service subscription that can be customized to your unique branding.

There are several popular services such as:

www.aweber.com

www.constantcontact.com

www.mailchimp.com

www.verticalresponse.com

Here is an easy five-step process to starting a company newsletter:

a. Pick your audience.

New customers? Market segment? Existing customers?

b. Choose what you're going to say.

Company news? Feature product? New offer?

c. Determine how you're going to say it.

Articles? Bullet points? Pictures?

d. Decide how it's going to get to your audience.

Email? Mail? In-store?

e. Track your results.

How many people opened it? Read it? Took action?

3. Value added service: give them happy surprises

Adding value to your business is an effective way of getting your customers back. Every person I know chooses a mattress store that offered free delivery over one that did not. It's that simple.

Think about your own buying patterns. When are you "happily surprised"? How does that impact your buying decision?

There are many ways to add value to your business, including:

a. Feature your expertise. Use your knowledge to provide additional value to your customers. Offer a free consumer guide or report with every purchase.

b. Add convenience services. Offer a service that makes their purchase easier or more convenient. The best example of this is free shipping or delivery.

c. Package complementary services. Packaging like items together creates an increase in perceived value. This is great for start-up kits.

d. Offer new products or services. Feature top of the line or exclusive products available only at your business. Offer a new service or profile a new team member with niche expertise.

4. **Value added services generate repeat customers in one of two ways:**

   a. <u>Impress them on their first visit</u>. Impress you customer with great service, a product that meets their needs, and then wow them with something extra that they weren't expecting. Get them to associate the experience of dealing with your business with happy surprises, and create a perception of higher value.

   b. <u>Entice them to come back</u>. The introduction of a new value-added service can be enough to convince a customer to buy from you again. Their initial purchase established a trust and knowledge of your business and its processes. They will want to "be included" in anything new that you have to offer – especially if there is exclusivity. It is easier to re-attract clients that have purchased from you than potential clients who have not.

5. **Customer loyalty programs: give them incentives**

Another simple way to keep in touch with existing customers and keep them coming back to you is to create a customer loyalty program.

These programs do not have to be complicated or costly and are relatively easy to maintain once they have been implemented. These programs help you gain more information on your customers and their purchasing habits.

Here are some examples of simple loyalty programs that you can implement:

a. <u>Free product or service</u>. Give them every 10th (or 6th) product or service free. Produce stamp cards with your logo and contact information on it.

b. <u>Reward dollars</u>. Give them a certain percentage of their purchase back in money that can only be spent in-store. Produce "funny money" with your logo and brand.

c. <u>Rewards points</u>. Give them a certain number of points for every dollar they spend. These points can be spent in-store, or on special items you bring in for points only.

d. <u>Membership amenities</u>. Give members access to VIP amenities that are not available to other customers. Produce member cards or give out member numbers.

e. <u>List additional ideas</u>

    i. _____

    ii. _____

    iii. _____

    iv. _____

Action Questions from Chapter 7

A. Value of Your Existing Customers?

What is the value of your existing customers?

B. Love Buying From You

Why do your customers love buying form you?

C. Keep In Touch

How do you keep in touch with your customers?

D. Value Added Services

What value added services do you provide?

E. Loyalty Programs

What loyalty programs do your competitors use?

What loyalty programs would work for your business?

F. Next Step

What "doable" next step will facilitate significant business results?

8

Double Your Referrals

Benefits of Referral Business

What if I told you that you could put an inexpensive system in place that would effectively allow your business to growth itself?

For most business owners, a large part of their customer base is comprised of referral customers. These people found out about the company's products or services from the recommendation of a friend or colleague who had a positive experience purchasing from that company.

If your business benefits from referral customers, you will find that these customers arrive ready to buy from you, and tend to buy more often. They also tend to be highly loyal to your product or service.

Referral customers are great customers to have. Referral customers impact your revenue, your expenses and your profits. Referral customers cost less to acquire. Compared to the leads you generate from advertising, direct mail campaigns, and other marketing initiatives, referral customers come to you already qualified and already trusting in the quality of your offering and the respectability of your team.

With a little effort, and the creation of a formalized system – or strategy – you can not only continue to enjoy referral business, but easily double the number of referral customers that walk through your door. All of this is possible for a minimal investment of time and resources.

Is Your Business a Referral Business?

Referral based businesses benefit from a stream of qualified customers who arrive at their doorstep ready to spend. These businesses put less focus on advertising to generate new leads, and more focus on serving and communicating with their existing customers.

Generally speaking, a referral program can generate outstanding results for nearly any business. Since most referrals do not require any effort, the addition of a strategy and a program will often double or triple the number of qualified referrals that come through a business's door.

There are, however, a few types of businesses that will not benefit from a formalized referral strategy. These are businesses with low price points – like fast food restaurants and drugstores. Their customer base is large already, and their efforts are best spent on increasing the average sale.

A referral program can:

1. **Save you time**

   Referral strategies – once established – don't require much management or time investment.

2. **Deliver more qualified customers**

   Your customer arrives with an assumption of trust and a willing to purchase.

3. **Improve your reputation**

   Your customer's networks likely overlap and create potential for a single customer to be referred by two people. This encourages the perception that your business is "the place to go."

4. **Speed the sales process**

   You will have existing common ground and a reputation with the referred customer.

5. **Increase your profit**

   You will spend less time and money generating leads, and more time serving customers who have their wallets open.

The Cost of Your Customers

As we discussed in the "Repeat Business" section, you don't "get" customers, you *buy* them. The money you spend on advertising, direct mail, and other promotions ideally results in potential customers walking through your doors.

For example, if you placed an ad for $200, and 20 people make a purchase in response to that ad, you would have paid $10 for each customer.

Referral customers cost you next to nothing. Your existing customer does the work of selling your business to their friend or associate, and you benefit from the sale. Aside from the cost of any referral incentives or coupon production, there is no cost involved at all.

Referral customers cost less and require less time investment than any other customer. That means you can spend that time making them a loyal customer or a devoted fan.

Groom Your Customers

Referral strategies can allow you to groom your customer base. As we have previously discussed, 80% of your revenue comes from 20% of your customers – these are your ideal customers.

These are also the people you have established as your target market, and are the people you cater your marketing and advertising efforts toward.

You also have a group of customers who make up 80% of your headaches. These are the people who complain the most and spend the least.

Use your referral strategy to get more of your *ideal* customers. Spend more time servicing your ideal customers – do everything you can to make them happy – and less time on your headache customers. You can even ask your headache customers to shop elsewhere.

Then, focus your referral efforts on your ideal customers. Ask them to refer business to you, and reward them for doing so. Try to avoid referrals from your headache customers – chances are that you'll just get another headache.

Referral Sources

Take some time to brainstorm all the people who could potentially refer business to you. Think beyond your business to your extracurricular activities and personal life. There are endless sources of people who are ready and willing to send potential customers your way. Here are some ideas to get you started:

1. Past relationships

No, not romantic relationships. I'm talking about anyone you have previously had a relationship with, but for one reason or another have fallen out of touch. This includes former colleagues, associates, customers, and friends.

Including them in your referral strategy can be as simple as reaching out through the phone or email, and updating them on your latest business initiative or career move. Gently ask at the end of the correspondence to refer anyone who may need your product or service. They will appreciate that you have attempted to re-establish the relationship.

2. Suppliers and vendors

Your suppliers and vendors can be a great source for referrals because they presumably deal daily with businesses that are complementary to your own. The opportunities to connect two of their customers in a mutually beneficial relationship are endless. These businesses should be happy to help out - especially if you have been a regular and loyal customer.

3. Customers

Customers are an obvious source of referrals because they are the people who are dealing with you directly on a regular basis. Often, all you have to do is ask and they will happily provide you with contact information of other interested buyers, or contact those buyers themselves.

Your customers also have a high level of product knowledge when it comes to your business, and are in a great position to really sell the strength of your company. Remember from the Testimonials section, the words of your customers are at least ten times more powerful than any clever headline or marketing piece you can create.

4. Employees and associates

Give your employees and associates a reason to have their friends and families shop at your business with a simple incentive program. These people have the most product knowledge, and are in the best position to sell you to a potential customer.

This is also a way to tap into an endless network of people. Who do your employees and associates know? Who do their friends and friends of friends know? A referral chain that connects to your employees can be a highly powerful one. Give bonuses or other incentives to employees who merge their network with your own.

5. Competitors

This doesn't seem so obvious, but it can work. Your direct competitors are clearly not the ideal source for referrals. However, indirect competitors can refer their clients or potential clients to you if they cannot meet those clients' needs themselves.

For example, if you sell high end lighting fixtures, the low-budget lighting store down the street may be able to refer clients to you, and vice versa. You may wish to offer a finder's fee or incentive to establish this arrangement.

6. Your network

Don't be shy about asking your friends and family members for referrals. Too many people do not provide enough information to their inner circle about what they do or what their business does. This doesn't make sense, since these are the people who should be the most interested!

Take time to explain clearly what your business is all about, and what your point of difference is. Then just ask them if they know anyone who may benefit from what you are offering. You could even provide your friends and family with an incentive – a gift, a meal, or a portion of the sale.

7. Associations + special interest groups

This is another place you likely have a network of people who have limited knowledge about what you do or what your business does. The advantage here is that you have a group of people with similar beliefs and values in the same room.

8. The media

Unless a member of the media is a regular customer of yours, or you are in business to serve the media, this may not seem like an obvious choice either.

The opportunity here is to establish a relationship with an editor or journalist, and position yourself as an expert in your field or industry. Then, the next time they are writing a related story, they can ask to quote you and your opinion. When their audience reads the story, they will perceive your business as the industry leader.

Referral Strategies

A referral strategy is any system that you put into place to generate new leads through existing customers. The ideal way to do this is to create a system that runs itself! Here are some ideas for simple strategies that you can begin to implement into your business immediately.

1. Just ask

This may seem simple and obvious, but it's true. Be open with your customers and associates, and simply ask them if they can refer any of their friends or associates to you. Make it part of doing business with you, and your customers will grow to expect the question. Or let them know in advance that you'll be asking at a later date.

Remember that this can include potential customers – even if they don't buy from you. The reason they chose not to purchase may have nothing to do with your business; any person who has begun to or actually has done business with you can refer to you another person.

2. Offer incentives

When you speak to your customers, when you ask them for something, you typically try to answer the question "what's in it for me?" before they ask it.

The same is true when you ask your customers for a referral. Incentive-based referral strategies work wonders, and can easily be implemented as part of a customer loyalty program, or as part of your existing customer relations systems.

Consider offering customers who successfully refer clients to you discounts on products, free products or services, or gifts. Offer incentives relative to the number of referrals, or the success rate of each referral.

This can have a spin off effect, as your referral customers may become motivated to continue the referral chain. They too will be interested in the incentives you have provided, and tell their friends about your business.

3. Be proactive

The only way your referral program will work is if you put some effort into it and maintain some level of ongoing effort. Here are some ideas:

- Put a referral card or coupon in every shopping bag or email.

- Promote gift certificates during peak seasons.

- Offer free information seminars to existing customers, and ask them to bring a friend.

- Host a closed-door sale for your top twenty customers and their friends.

4. Provide great customer service

An easy way to encourage referral business is to treat every potential customer with exemplary customer service. Since the art of customer service is lost in many communities, people are often impressed by simple added touches and conveniences. That alone will encourage them to refer your business to their network.

5. Stay in touch

Make sure you are staying in touch with all of your potential and converted customers. Through newsletters, direct mail, or the Internet, keep your business name at the top of their minds, ahead of the competition.

Even if they have already purchased from you and may not need to purchase again for some time, a newsletter or email can be a simple reminder that your business is out there. If someone in their network is looking for the product or service, it will be more likely that your customer will refer your business over the competition.

Action Questions from Chapter 8

A. Value of a Referral Program

List three ways a referral program would benefit your business?

B. Current Customer Cost

How much do your current customers cost you?

C. Grooming Your Customers

How are your grooming your customers to provide referrals?

D. Referrals

Where your referrals have (past) come from?

Where your referrals will (future) come from?

E. Referral Strategies

List three referral strategies that you will implement.

F. Next Step

What "doable" next step will facilitate significant business results?

9

Reverse Risk to Increase Sales

Increase Your Competitive Edge

What is the biggest objection that you need to overcome when closing a sale? Is it cost? Belief in what you have to say? Confidence in your product or service?

While it is a different answer for every business, every business has to deal with some element of customer fear or hesitation before a monetary transaction can take place.

The reality is that even if you overcome these objections and close the sale, your customer walks away carrying 99% of the risk associated with the purchase. If the product doesn't work, breaks down, or doesn't perform to expectations, then your customer has parted with their dollars in exchange for disappointment.

In marketing, your objective is to generate as many leads as possible, then to convert each lead into a customer or sale. The ratio of leads to closed sales is called your conversion rate.

What if you could eliminate the risk involved in a transaction? Would you turn more leads into customers? The answer is absolutely yes.

Introducing a risk reversal element into your marketing message or unique offer is a powerful way to give yourself an edge over the competition and close more sales. But how exactly are you going to do this? It's easy, just give them a guarantee.

The Power of Guarantees

What is Risk Reversal?

Risk reversal simply refers to reversing the risk associated with a transaction – transferring it from the customer to the vendor.

Everyone can think of a handful of times that they have purchased a product or service that did not deliver on their expectations: a time where a salesperson made them a promise and did not deliver, a time where they *lost money* on a faulty product or bogus service.

Fear of being burned or taken advantage of prevents many people from spending their money. Customers can also be very wary of buying a product or service for the first time.

Providing a strong guarantee eliminates the majority of risk involved in the purchase, and breaks down natural barriers in the sales process. Guarantees will often shorten the sales process all together – skipping any discussion of objections – because the customer does not see any risk in "trying the product out."

There is also a growing consumer expectation when it comes to guarantees. Many stores take back anything the customer has not been happy with and return money or give store credit. Popular health food stores encourage customers to try new or unfamiliar products by promising a hassle-free, no questions asked return process. A guarantee or easy return policy can be the difference between choosing one business over its competition.

Your Customers Buy Results

The strongest guarantee you can make is on *results*, not products or services.

If you guarantee that your customer will receive the benefits or results they are looking for, the specific product or service they'll need to achieve those results becomes irrelevant.

People buy benefits and results. For example, they don't buy water purifiers; they buy the benefit of enjoying clean, fresh-tasting water. They don't buy lawn sprinkler systems; they buy a healthy green lawn.

Once you understand what specific benefit or solution your customers are seeking, find a way to guarantee they'll receive or experience that solution. If they don't, you'll compensate them for it.

Remember What You Have Guaranteed

While guarantees will increase sales for most businesses, they can also be the fast track to business failure if their product or service isn't a quality one. Take the time to ensure that you have a strong offering before you implement a guarantee.

Guarantees are most effective when you are selling someone something they need or want – not when you are trying to convince someone to purchase something that they have no use for.

Guarantees Increase Conversion Rates

Guarantees can help your business turn more qualified leads into repeat customers. Strong guarantees are big and bold, but also realistic. They're just a little bit better than your competition, but consistent with the industry's standards.

Your Conversion Rate

Your conversion rate is the percentage of clients you convert from leads into customers (# transactions / # leads x 100 = % conversion rate). The higher your conversion rate, the more revenue you will generate.

To figure out your conversion rate, divide the number of people who purchase from you by the number of people who inquired about your product or service. This will generate a percentage value for your conversion rate.

Guarantees encourage and increase conversion. They motivate potential customers to buy – and to buy from you – because you stand behind what you sell in a big way. There is no risk involved in purchasing what you have to offer.

Creating Your Guarantee

So you're convinced that your business – and your customers – will benefit from a strong guarantee. Now what? What are you going to guarantee? How are you going to position it?

Once again, this goes back to your target audience and your product or service. What are some of the major objections your potential customers raise during the sales process? What kind of risk do they take on when they make a purchase? How much time will they need to test or experience your product or service?

Brainstorm a list of things about your industry that really frustrate your customers. They could be service-based (contractors that don't show up, employees who don't perform) or product-based (products that break, do not perform). Then take a look at your list and decide how you can make sure these things do not happen. Think big – you can do a lot more than you think – then determine if you can actually make good on your promise. If you can't guarantee to overcome the first frustration, then move on to the second.

Here are some tips on writing your guarantee:

1. Be specific

Explain exactly what you are guaranteeing. Don't make vague guarantees that a product will "work" or that a service will make you "happy". These words mean different things to different people. Guarantee specific performances or results.

2. Include a clear timeframe

Put a realistic timeframe on your guarantee. Very few products or services are good forever. Offer a 30-day or 90-day free trial; guarantee results within a set number of days or weeks. This can protect your company, and sets out clear expectations for your clients.

3. Be bold

Unbelievable guarantees get a customer's attention, so go as far as you realistically can with your claim. Find a way to stand out over the competition – which may also have a guarantee.

4. Tell them what you'll do

Explain what you'll do – how you'll compensate them – if your product or service doesn't deliver. Be specific, talk money, and go above and beyond.

Implementing guarantees

1. Tell your clients!

Put your guarantee everywhere – your website, brochures, receipt tape, in-store signage, advertisements, and other promotional materials. It will only help attract customers if they know about it.

Send a newsletter to your existing client base informing them of your new guarantees – you never know how many customers you can convince to come back and spend more in your business.

2. Train your team

Once you have decided to offer your clients a guarantee, you need to ensure your team are properly trained on the specific policies and procedures associated with that guarantee. If you offer different guarantees for different products and services, ensure this is made clear, as well.

Presumably, your team will be communicating the details of your guarantee and fielding customer questions. They will have to know how to sell the product using the guarantee as a benefit, and understand every application of the guarantee in your business, every scenario a customer may need to use it.

To ensure your team is not making any false claims or promises, create a guarantee script for them to use and stick to. This prevents customers from returning with false hopes for their money back, or other compensation.

Returns + Claims

So by now you must be thinking, "Great, I can convert more customers with a strong guarantee, and increase my sales. But what about the added risk I have taken on from my customers? Won't I start to see a ton of returns and service claims?" This is a valid question. Making a strong guarantee means standing by it and delivering on your promise. Inevitably, when you guarantee something, someone is going to take you up on that guarantee and make a claim. I'm going to answer this question in two parts:

1. **Stand behind your product or service**

You're not in business to scam customers. If you sell a product or service and you believe in it enough to offer it to your customers, it is likely a quality product or genuine service.

If this is a concern to you, consider implementing strong quality controls or stronger criteria for your merchandising. Companies that offer products and services that deliver results can offer the strongest guarantees.

Of course, you will get returns. You will have customers come in to take advantage of you. Just remember that as long as the increase in sales outweighs the claims, your guarantee strategy has been successful.

Consider your tolerance for risk and your ability to provide follow-up. Unhappy customers tell at least nine people about their experience.

2. Understand your customers (likely behavior)

The truth is that most customers will never take advantage of your guarantee – regardless of their satisfaction level. There are a number of reasons for this.

The first is that most people can't be bothered to drive, mail, or otherwise seek a refund on an item under $50. Many let the timeframe slip by and have an "oh well" attitude.

The second is that most people don't like confrontation. There is usually an element of confrontation involved in telling someone you didn't like a product or service, and many people do not have the confidence to do so. They'd rather eat the cost than go through the process of asking for a refund.

Handling Claims and Returns

If you do have your product returned, it is in your company's best interest to create a system for handling these customer interactions.

1. Create a claim form

Ensure that each customer who makes a claim about your product or service fills out a standard form. Doing so will help you prevent fraud, gather important information about the customer and their reasoning, and create a "hoop" for the customer to jump through if they want their money back. It also helps you track the reasoning behind the returns, making it easier in the future to prevent the setbacks that necessitated the return, and maybe helping you formulate new guarantees that can overcome these setbacks.

Date:	
Name:	
Contact Information:	
Sales Person:	
Sales Method:	
Sales Date:	
Product:	
Service:	
Reason for Claim:	
Comments:	
Follow-Up:	

Keep a claim or return log

Create an electronic system for your claims. This will give you a snapshot of your guarantee program, a record-keeping system, and a wealth of information about each customer's experience and motivations. The claims and returns system should be linked to your primary customer database.

Use The Information

Take the claim forms your customers have filled out and review them regularly. While some of the claims won't be genuine, there will be some real feedback you can use to improve your product or service, or to modify your guarantee. You may need to make it more realistic, or change the specifics.

Action Questions from Chapter 9

A. Biggest Objections

What major objections do your customers pose during a sale?

B. Addressing Objections

What can you do you eliminate objections?

Action Questions from Chapter 9

C. Top Guarantee

What is your top guarantee?

D. Implement Guarantee

How will you implement your guarantee?

E. Claim Policies

What are your return and claim policies?

F. Reversing Risk

What do you need to do to reverse your risk?

G. Increasing Sales/Reducing Claims

What do you need to do to increase your sales?

What do you need to do to reduce your claims?

H. Next Steps

What "doable" next step will facilitate significant business results?

10

Create Added Value

Retain Existing and Attract New

The majority of small businesses, like yours, are established in response to market demand for a products or services. Many build their businesses by serving that demand, and enjoy growing profits without putting much effort into long-term planning or marketing.

However, what happens when that demand slows or stops? What happens when the competition sets up shop with a "new and improved" version of your product down the road? How do you keep your offering fresh, while growing and maintaining your client base? The answer is by adding value to your product or service.

Added value is a marketing or customer relations strategy that can take the form of a product or service that is added to the original offering for free, or as part of a discounted package. It, like all other elements in your marketing toolkit, is designed to attract new customers and retain existing ones. A simple example of added value is if you owned a gift shop and offered complimentary gift wrapping with every purchase.

If you don't refresh and renew your offering over time, your customers will get bored and be drawn to your competitor. Your employees, too, may become disinterested, and find work elsewhere. Ultimately, both clients and employees will demand additional value to remain loyal – and aren't they the keystones for your business growth?

Can You Add Value to Your Business?

Everyone can add value to their business. Better yet, everyone can *afford* to add value to their business. Adding value doesn't have to blow your marketing budget, or take up hours of your time. There are many ways – big and small – to enhance your business in the eyes of your clients.

The key to adding value is determining what your customers and target market perceive as valuable. You must understand their needs, wants, troubles, and inconveniences in order to entice them with solutions through added value products or services. Adding value will add to your profits, but if you don't focus on genuinely helping your clients, you'll have a difficult time attracting them.

Added value works for both product- and service-based businesses. If you offer a service, like hairstyling, try treating your customers with products like a latte while they wait, shampoo samples, or a free conditioning treatment with every sixth visit. If you sell a product, consider offering convenience services – like free shipping or delivery – to make the customer's experience a seamless one. The customer will feel appreciated and their needs will have been taken care of.

Ways to Add Value to Your Business

There are many ways to enhance your offer, depending on your budget and the resources you have access to. You may wish to hold a brainstorming session with your team to come up with ideas for your business; if your employees are on the front lines, they'll likely have firsthand information about what clients want to see more of.

1. Feature your expertise

Your intellectual property is a free resource that you have at your disposal to share with your clients. This will make them feel as though they have an inside track. You might want to consider adding it to your business, making it a value-added service.

2. Expert corner

Supplement your website and newsletter with columns on topics of interest to your customers and of relevance to your service. This will position you as an expert in the marketplace, and give your clients helpful information.

3. Do it yourself tips

This is a great tool for seasonal marketing. Provide your clients with this information on your website, in your newsletters, or on take away note cards in your store or office. Ideas include recipes, craft ideas, gift ideas – all of which are branded with your company logo and contact information, and include your product as an ingredient.

4. What to expect tips

Take your customer through what they should expect in the first few days (weeks) of using your service or product, and how they can make the most of it. This can include assembly instructions, product care and cleaning, or service results (like a 25% increase in business – guaranteed!).

5. Related and community events

Own a store that sells athletic equipment? Post information on your website, in store, and in your newsletter about upcoming races, games, or consumer trade shows. Or simply keep a bulletin in your office of community events and offers that will draw your clients in and establish the store as a hub in the neighborhood for information.

6. Offer convenience services

Customer service is a dying practice in our high paced culture – use it to your advantage. When done well, it can be the difference between you and the competition, or the deciding factor for a potential repeat client.

Make it Easy for Your Customers

Envision the steps involved for a customer to arrive at your store, purchase your offering, and use your product or service. Can you eliminate any of those steps for them? Can you shorten waiting times or make them more pleasurable? Stepping into your clients' shoes allows you to determine the most powerful value add for your company. Here are a few ideas:

1. Free delivery + shipping

With clearly established parameters (will you ship your product free to India?), this is a solid value added service that many businesses offer. Free delivery (usually with a purchase over a set amount) is a huge convenience for many people who do not have access to a vehicle or who need help moving large items.

2. Follow-up services

This works great for computers, appliances, and other mechanical or technology-based products. Offer maintenance and service contracts for three time periods; instead of dealing with the manufacturer, customers will rely on you for assistance, which brings them back into the store and establishes a relationship of trust.

3. Gift-wrapping

A great service to provide – especially for seasonal gifts. This service costs very little, and can have a big impact on your customer's experience.

4. "While you wait" amenities

If you could make your customer feel like a VIP for minimal cost, why wouldn't you? Offering amenities like coffee and treats, free samples, and services (wireless internet is a big one) will go a long way.

5. Comparison-shopping tools

Show your customers that you are so sure that your product will measure up against the competition that you'll help them compare.

Establish Complementary Partnerships

Complementary partnerships with other businesses can take you a long way toward adding value for your customer and generating new business. Just like a joint testimonial mailing, the power (and convenience) of referral business is immense.

1. Build a web of associates

If you're a yoga instructor, carry the cards of your treatment providers (physiotherapists, massage therapists, etc.) to refer your students to. In exchange, your brochure or card is posted in your providers' offices. This works for automotive repair, esthetics, consultants, and other service providers. Customers will trust referrals received by their existing service providers and feel taken care of by a reputable community of experts.

2. Establish partnerships with financial incentives

This is one that has your interests in mind, as well as your customers'. In addition to establishing a complementary partnership with a related associate, establish an incentive structure where each of you are compensated for your referrals. For example, if you refer a client to a furniture store after they've purchased a mattress from you, and they buy a bed frame, your associate pays you a portion of the sale – and vice versa.

3. Location-based partnerships

Consider creating partnerships with the businesses around you – even if your products and services don't appear to be related. Shopping malls do this all the time with value coupon books that customers must purchase for $5 to $20 dollars. These partnerships and incentives will keep the customer spending money in the area, which is good for everyone's bottom line.

Packages + Bundles

Packaging and bundling products and services is one of the most popular methods of adding value. Clients perceive the bundles as having a higher value than the sum of the individual items – or as receiving something for free.

Cleverly packaged and named bundles can spark interest and revive your products in the eyes of your customers. Remember to always give the offers an end date or provide a limited number to create a sense of scarcity and urgency and to prevent this strategy from going stale.

1. Intuitive product bundles

Package independent related products together, and give them a reduced price or name. For example, this could be selling an extra pair of running socks with new running shoes. Remember the convenience of starter kits – package everything your customer will need to begin a new activity – painting, camping, running, etc. – in a bundle for simple buying decisions.

2. Package your up-sell

This can also be called a chain of purchasing. It includes the products or services your client will need to use your product or service. Won't they need leather protector for their new boots? If they've run out of oil paints, how's their supply of brushes, acrylics or canvases?

By packaging these clearly related products together, you are making their shopping experience faster and more convenient.

Offer a Customer Loyalty Program

There are a number of ways to structure your rewards and loyalty program, depending on the type of business and level of technological resources available to you. Customer loyalty programs have a huge advantage – they help build your database of customer information, and in most cases allow you to view and analyze purchasing patterns. Here are the most popular:

1. Every 6th (or 10th) visit on us

This works well for business that rely on repeat visits from their customers – like hair salons, coffee shops, auto maintenance, etc. Customers receive a card with store information on the front, and space for stamps or initials on the back. Remember that while ten is a nice even number, it may be too far in the future for some customers (especially for services that are three to six weeks apart). The idea of six visits is more manageable.

2. Rewards dollars

This is the Canadian Tire model. For every dollar your customer spends in store, they receive a small portion back in store credit (i.e.,

Canadian Tire money). The store credit is in the form of printed dollars, branded with your company logo and contact information, and serves as a reminder each time a client opens their wallet.

3. Rewards points

Another common value-add strategy is a rewards points system. Most grocery stores use this incentive, as well as credit card companies. This works the same as rewards dollars, where a certain number of points are accumulated based on each dollar spent in store. Points can then be spent in store, or on products you have brought in for "rewards points holders" only. This strategy also allows you to feature products with "extra points value" instead of discounting prices.

4. Membership amenities

Instead of points or dollars, you can offer VIP treatment for members, when they sign up for or purchase a membership. This may include occasional discounts, but is primarily centered around perks like "while you wait" amenities, skipping the line, free delivery, etc. You can also produce membership cards.

5. List additional ideas

a. _____

b. _____

Action Questions from Chapter 10

A. Adding Value

How will you add value in your business?

B. Making It Easy

How you will make it easy for your customers?

C. Complimentary Partnerships

How you will you establish complementary partnerships?

D. Your Package/Bundle

What you would put in your package or bundle?

E. Customer Loyalty Program

What you will offer in your customer loyalty program?

How will you update your loyalty program?

F. Next Step

What "doable" next step will facilitate significant business results?

Chapter Summaries

Business Results Checklist

1.   **Define Your Target Market**

2.   **Create a Powerful Offer**

3.   **Use Testimonials for Social Proof**

4.   **Create Unlimited Leads**

5.   **Create Immediate Sales**

6.   **Use Scripts to Increase Sales**

7.   **Create Repeat Business**

8.   **Double Your Referrals**

9.   **Reverse Risk to Increase Sales**

10.   **Create Added Value**

Chapter Summary - 1

Define Your Target Market

1. A target market is the group of customers or clients who will purchase a specific product or service. This group has something in common (age, gender, hobbies, location, industry, etc.).

2. Your target market are the existing and potential customers who will buy your offering. They are motivated to do one of three things:
    1. Fulfill a need
    2. Solve a problem
    3. Satisfy a desire

3. Knowledge and understanding of your target market is the keystone in the arch of your business. Without it, your product or service positioning, pricing, and marketing strategy fall apart.

4. Determining your target market takes time and careful diligence. While it often starts with a best guess, assumptions cannot be relied on and research is required to confirm original ideas. Your target market is not always your ideal market.

5. Your market segments are the groups within your target market – broken down by a variable in one of the following four categories:
    - Demographics
    - Psychographics
    - Geographics
    - Behaviors

6. Segmenting your target market into several more specific groups allows you to further tailor your marketing campaign and more specifically position your product or service.

7. Learn everything you can about your target market. You need to have a strong understanding of who they are, what they like, where they shop, why they buy, and how they spend their time.

Chapter Summary - 2

Create a Powerful Offer

1. Your offer is the granite foundation of your marketing campaign. Get it right and everything else will fall into place. Your headline will grab readers, your copy will sing, your ad layout will hardly matter, and you will have customers running to your door.

2. The powerful offer is more often than not the reason a customer will open their wallets. It is how you generate leads and then convert them into loyal customers. The more dramatic, unbelievable, and valuable the offer is, the more dramatic and unbelievable the responses will be.

3. A powerful offer is one that makes the most people respond, and take action. It gets people running to spend money on your product or service.

4. Powerful offers nearly always have an element of urgency and of scarcity. They give your audience a reason to act immediately, instead of putting it off until a later date.

5. Decide what kind of offer will most effectively achieve your objectives. Are you trying to generate leads, convert customers, build a database, move old product off the shelves, or increase sales?

6. Create a powerful offer in four steps:
   - Pick a single product or service
   - Decide what you want your customers to do
   - Dream up the biggest, best offer
   - Run the numbers

Chapter Summary - 3

Use Testimonials for Social Proof

1. Testimonials are simply the single most powerful asset you can have in your marketing toolkit. When your customers tell others about the benefits of choosing your business, it is a thousand times more powerful than the same words from your mouth.

2. By asking a customer for a testimonial, you are asking for their assistance in the growth of your business. When they feel they are truly helping and participating in your company, their sense of pride will mean continuous loyalty to your product or service.

3. 11 ways to get great testimonials:
   - Don't wait
   - Get specific
   - If you were the solution - what was the problem?
   - Write the first draft
   - Include your marketing message or USP
   - A picture says...
   - Credentials equal trust
   - Don't forget to ask permission
   - Location, location…
   - Testimonials are not surveys
   - Say thank you!

4. Strategies for putting testimonials to use:
   - Put them on your website
   - Compile your best 25 - 50 letters in a display book
   - Hang your favorite testimonials in your store or office
   - Put them in your advertisements
   - Include a page of testimonials in your direct mail
   - Partner with an associate for a joint mailing

Chapter Summary - 4

Create Unlimited Leads

1. Your customers come from leads that have been turned into sales. Each customer goes through a process before they arrive with their wallets open. They have been converted from a member of a target market, to a lead, then to a customer.

2. The first step towards increasing your leads is understanding how many leads you currently get on a regular basis, as well as where they come from.

3. The ratio of leads (potential customers) to transactions (actual customers) is called your conversion rate. Simply divide the number of customers who actually purchased something by the number of customers who inquired about your product or service, and multiply by 100.

4. Quality leads are the people who are the most likely to buy your product or service. They are the qualified buyers who comprise your target market.

5. Marketing and customer outreach for the purpose of lead generation can be inexpensive and bring a high return on investment.

6. A referral system is one of the most profitable systems you can create in your business. Once it's set up, it often runs itself.

7. Once your lead generation strategies are in place, you'll also need a system to manage incoming inquiries. You'll need to ensure that you receive enough information from each lead to follow-up on at a later date. You'll also need to create a system to organize that information and track the lead as it is converted into a sale.

Chapter Summary - 5

Create Immediate Sales

1. The ability to sell effectively and efficiently is one every successful business owner has cultivated and continues to develop. Selling may be complicated and time consuming. You have to continually work on it to be and stay successful.

2. The sales process varies according to the type of business, type of customers, and type of product or service that is offered; however, the core steps are the same.

3. The Seven Step Sales Process:
   - Preparation
   - Build a relationship
   - Discuss needs + wants
   - Present the solution
   - Overcome objections
   - Close
   - Service + follow-up

4. Up-selling is simply inviting your customers to spend more money in your business by purchasing additional products or services. This can include more of the same product, complementary products, or impulse items.

5. Effective management of your sales team is a skill every business owner should cultivate.

6. Every salesperson should have an arsenal of tools and aids to assist them in the sales process, to help to foster continual learning and skill development of skills.

Chapter Summary - 6

Use Scripts to Increase Sales

1. A large number of businesses use scripts to maintain consistency among a sales team, train new salespeople, or enhance their sales skills. They may have a single script or several, and may change their scripts regularly.

2. If you are not using scripts, you're only working at half of your true potential, or making half of your potential earnings.

3. Scripts are like any other element of your marketing campaign, they need to be tested and measured for results and changed based on what is or is not working.

4. Creating powerful scripts is not a complicated exercise, but it will take some time to complete. Focus on the most vital scripts for your business first and engage the assistance of your sales team in drafting or reviewing the scripts.

5. Keep master copies of all of your scripts in one, organized place. Create a binder with tabs for each script.

6. Six Steps to Successful Scripts:
   - Record what you're doing now
   - Evaluate what you're doing wrong
   - Decide who the script is for
   - Decide what you want to say
   - Train your team
   - Continually revise

Chapter Summary - 7

Create Repeat Business

1. Successful businesses that see sustained growth have a double-edged marketing strategy. They focus their efforts outward – on potential customers and marketing – as well as inward – on existing customers and referral business.

2. These successful businesses have leveraged their existing efforts to generate more revenue. Simply put, their customers buy from them over and over again.

3. Each new customer that walks through your door – with the exception of referrals – has cost you money to acquire. You have spent money on advertising and promotions to generate leads and turn those leads into customers.

4. Generating more repeat business means focusing on the marketing strategies that aim to keep your existing customers instead of purchasing new ones – effectively reducing the cost of attracting new customers to your business.

5. Marketing strategies that focus on keeping your current customer base are easy and enjoyable to implement. They allow you to build real relationships with the people you do business with, instead of dealing with a revolving door of people on the other end of your sales process.

6. In order for the customer loyalty programs to work, you and your team have to understand and promote it.

7. Get clients to pay, stay and refer.

Chapter Summary - 8

Double Your Referrals

1. For most business owners, a large part of their customer base is comprised of referral customers. These people found out about the company's products or services from the recommendation of a friend or colleague who had a positive experience purchasing from that company.

2. With a little effort, and the creation of a formalized system – or strategy – you can not only continue to enjoy referral business, but easily double the number of referral customers that walk through your door, all for a minimal investment of time and resources.

3. Generally speaking, a referral program can generate outstanding results for nearly any business. Since most referrals do not require any effort, the addition of a strategy and a program will often double or triple the number of qualified referrals that come through a business door.

4. Take some time to brainstorm all the people who could potentially refer business to you. Think beyond your business, to your extracurricular activities and personal life. There are endless sources of people who are ready and willing to send potential customers your way.

5. A referral strategy is any system that you can put in place to generate new leads through existing customers. The program in itself becomes a product that you sell. The ideal way to do this is to create a system that runs itself!
    *   Just ask
    *   Offer incentives
    *   Be proactive
    *   Provide great customer service
    *   Stay in touch

Chapter Summary - 9

Reverse Risk to Increase Sales

1. Introducing a risk reversal element into your marketing message or unique offer is a powerful way to get an edge on the competition and close more sales.

2. Providing a strong guarantee eliminates the majority of risk involved in the purchase and breaks down natural barriers in the sales process. Guarantees will often shorten the sales process altogether, skipping any discussion of objections, because the customer does not see any risk in "trying the product out."

3. The strongest guarantee you can make is on results, not products or services.

4. Guarantees can help your business turn more qualified leads into repeat customers. Strong guarantees are big and bold, but also realistic. They're just a little bit better than your competition, but consistent with the industry's standards.

5. Here are some tips on writing your guarantee:
   - Be specific
   - Include a clear timeframe
   - Be bold
   - Tell them what you'll do

6. Making a strong guarantee means standing by it and delivering on your promise. Inevitably, when you guarantee something, someone is going to take you up on that guarantee and make a claim.

7. If you do have your product returned, it is in your company's best interest to create a system for handling these customer interactions.

Chapter Summary - 10

Create Added Value

1. Retain existing customers and attract new customers.

2. Most small businesses are established in response to market demand for a product or service. Many build their businesses by serving that demand and enjoy growing profits without putting much effort into long-term planning or marketing.

3. Added value is a marketing or customer relations strategy that can take the form of a product, service, that is added to the original offering for free, or as part of a discounted package. It, like all other elements in your marketing toolkit, is designed to attract new customers and retain existing ones.

4. Everyone can add value to your business and it doesn't have to blow your marketing budget, or take up hours of your time.

5. The key to adding value is determining what your customers and target market perceive as valuable. You must understand their needs, wants, troubles, and inconveniences in order to entice them with solutions through added value products or services. Adding value will add to your profits, but if you don't focus on genuinely helping your clients, you'll have a difficult time attracting them.

6. Five main ways to add value to your business are:
    *   Feature Your Expertise
    *   Offer Convenience Services
    *   Establish Complementary Partnerships
    *   Packages + Bundles
    *   Offer a Customer Loyalty Program

Start Now!

If you're already an accomplished business owner and earning in excess of $250,000 per year (rich according to the federal government), use this book to significantly enhance the speed of your business success.

If you are not as accomplished as you want to be, then:

a.   Use the strategies to learn and earn!
b.   Follow advice and take action!
c.   Work smart and the start will be easier!
d.   Test and track so you know what worked well!

If you are serious about taking the next step, then go to work on yourself, study other business successes, understand marketing strategies, and become a sponge for new (proven) material. The amazing thing about the game of business is that when you put proven processes to work and continue to follow them, an abundance of success follows. The biggest mistake is to start a process and then fallback into your old habits after a short time. Above all, get the knowledge you need.

If you were going to challenge Michael Jordan to a game of basketball for money, wouldn't it make sense to learn the game and practice before you stepped on the court to play him?

It's amazing to me how many small business people intentionally put themselves at a disadvantage against seasoned professionals (the competition), because they don't want to first develop the necessary knowledge to be successful. Then after they fail, they blame the market, the economy, their location, etc.

If you want to start to create wealth and systems that allow you to take time off, build retirement accounts, or pay for your children's college, then learn and master the steps outlined in my book. I am a huge advocate of education and mentorships. Get the right information, find someone that knows how to walk you through them, and watch your quality of life take new shape.

Significantly yours in success,

Franne McNeal, MBA
Significant Business Results Coach
Franne@SBizResults.com
www.SBizResults.com

Are you ready to increase your sales, cash flow and profits?

Hire a Significant Business Results Coach.
Get faster and smarter business growth.

Acquire the best marketing resources at www.SBizResults.com
Bonus: Seven-day access to a business building membership site.

Coaching Clients Feedback

Franne McNeal

Significant Business Reviews

Entrepreneurs and Leaders value Franne McNeal, Business Coach

VALUE PROPOSITION

Confidential CEO Support

Seasoned External Perspective

Minimize Risks

Maximize Performance

Strategic Investment

Balanced Scorecard ROI

Organizational Dashboard

Stakeholder Focused

Leadership Team Development

"You helped me make sense of unfinished pieces that had been running in my head. Our coaching sessions helped me gain significant contracts." Karen Hinds

"Franne is an excellent business coach. She helped me develop my first business plan. I doubled my earnings the year after I worked with Franne." Margot Friedman

"Franne has a great skill of looking outside of your situation to come up with a creative solution. After a brief coaching call with Franne, I had new plan and strategy to implement. In 30 minutes she helped me get clarity on an issue that I had been struggling with for months." Jennifer Dent, M.S.

"I was so impressed with Franne's skills that I engaged her to help me develop my business growth plan. Franne is personable, extremely results-oriented, well-organized and creative. She has a strong analytic and strategic approach to business development. Sara Robins

"Franne did an amazing job of seeing what is needed in my business and very quickly helped me to prioritize and address the issues." Robert Joseph, Ph.D.

www.frannemcneal.com

Coaching Clients Results

Franne McNeal

COACHING SERVICES

Executive Coaching

CEO MasterMind Group

Strategic Planning

Group Coaching

Organization-Wide Summit

Significant Business Results

Client Case Studies

Increased Sales
Owner of a professional services firm, frustrated by a 20% decrease in sales in the past two years.
Coaching results: Three new strategic partnerships, including a two-year contract valued at $1,000,000.

Private Sector Contracts
Owner of a specialty food product business wanted to double her sales from 1.5 million dollars to 3 million dollars.
Coaching results: Obtained a new contract of $400,000.

Federal Contracts
Minority owned information technology firm needed to leverage expertise to win government contracts.
Coaching results: Company awarded a $3 million contract.

Performance to Profitability
Owner of a training firm wanted to refresh her brand, market a premium service, and add trainers.
Coaching results: Branding project completed in 60 days, and premium service sales increased by 300%.

Investor Presentation
Manufacturer of baby clothes needed funding for equipment, and working capital.
Coaching results: Honed investor presentations, which resulted in equipment, capital, resources and advisors.

www.frannemcneal.com

166

Coaching Process

Franne McNeal

COACHING PROCESS

Complimentary Consultation

Assessments

Results Discovery

Coaching Contract

Coaching Services

Monthly Metrics Review

Quarterly Metrics Review

Semi-Annual Metrics Review

Annual Metrics Review

About Coach Franne

Franne McNeal
Entrepreneur
Business Coach

www.frannemcneal.com

Significant!
"Franne models what she preaches.
Disciplined yet flexible, creative yet practical.
She delivers brilliant and valuable solutions."
Margie Strosser, Consultant

Franne McNeal, helps entrepreneurs achieve significant business results. Franne works with businesses positioned to generate $50M in annual revenues through values-based leadership and a vision of sustainability.

Clients choose Significant Business Results Coach Franne McNeal, because she creates strategies, leverages teams and monitors results for increased sales, improved cash flow, reduced expenses, and greater profitability. In the last 12 years, over 10,000 entrepreneurs have grown their businesses based on her proprietary coaching system: The Business PeaPod™.

Franne's clients have been featured in Black Enterprise Magazine, Business Week, Entrepreneur Magazine, Forbes, Inc Magazine, The New York Times, and The Wall Street Journal; as well as major TV and cable networks.

Franne McNeal is a serial entrepreneur, keynote speaker, author, and business plan competition judge. She is a certified Kauffman Foundation FastTrac Facilitator, and Adjunct Faculty for the Goldman Sachs 10,000 Small Businesses Initiative.

Franne McNeal earned a BA from Princeton University, and a MBA from Eastern University. She has received numerous professional awards. She is the volunteer host for The BDPA iRadio Show and an avid gardener.

Keynote Speaking Feedback

Franne McNeal

Passion
Purpose
Profitability

Rave Reviews for Franne McNeal
Entrepreneur and Keynote Speaker

POPULAR WORKSHOPS

Vision, Values, Vitality

Size, Scale, Sustain

Possibility to Profitability

People, Process, Performance

Passion, Purpose, Profitability

Maximize, Minimize, Modify

Grow Your Small Biz

Cash Flow: Sink or Swim

"Franne is Franne-tastic! She is well organized, thoughtful and funny. She synthesizes information brilliantly and makes it palpable. A great presence!"
John Benton, Producer/Screenwriter

"Franne brought energy, knowledge and impeccable comedic timing to a potentially too serious and often complicated subject. I strongly recommend Franne."
Bruce Marsh, Consultant

"It is unusual and tremendously gratifying to find someone who can communicate that knowledge with clarity, wit and ease. Franne teaches by showing, as much as telling."
Laine Zera, Founder

"Franne commanded the room and our attention. She is high energy, inspiring and no-nonsense. All the attributes you want in a speaker."
Adele Finer, AIA, LEED AP

"Franne enlightens and empowers through superb communication skills and extensive business knowledge. She is a wonderful speaker who succinctly gets to the core of how to make a good decision."
Celina Guerrero, Director

www.frannemcneal.com

169

About Keynote Speaker Franne

www.frannemcneal.com

Franne McNeal
Entrepreneur
Keynote Speaker

Franne McNeal, helps entrepreneurs achieve significant business results. Franne works with businesses positioned to generate $50M in annual revenues through values-based leadership and a vision of sustainability.

Clients choose Significant Business Results Coach Franne McNeal, because she creates strategies, leverages teams and monitors results for increased sales, improved cash flow, reduced expenses, and greater profitability. In the last 12 years, over 10,000 entrepreneurs have grown their businesses based on her proprietary coaching system: The Business PeaPod™.

Franne's clients have been featured in Black Enterprise Magazine, Business Week, Entrepreneur Magazine, Forbes, Inc Magazine, The New York Times, and The Wall Street Journal; as well as major TV and cable networks.

Franne McNeal is a serial entrepreneur, keynote speaker, author, and business plan competition judge. She is a certified Kauffman Foundation FastTrac Facilitator, and Adjunct Faculty for the Goldman Sachs 10,000 Small Businesses Initiative.

Franne McNeal earned a BA from Princeton University, and a MBA from Eastern University. She has received numerous professional awards. She is the volunteer host for The BDPA iRadio Show and an avid gardener.

www.ingramcontent.com/pod-product-compliance
Lightning Source LLC
Chambersburg PA
CBHW070400200326
41518CB00011B/2006